Modernization of Human Resource Traditions

Nirmalendu Mohapatra

Viva Books

New Delhi | Mumbai | Chennai | Kolkata | Bengaluru | Hyderabad | Kochi | Guwahati

Publisher's note

Every possible effort has been made to ensure that the information contained in this book is accurate at the time of going to press, and the publisher and author cannot accept responsibility for any errors or omissions, however caused. No responsibility for loss or damage occasioned to any person acting, or refraining from action, as a result of the material in this publication can be accepted by the editor, the publisher or the author.

Every effort has been made to trace the owners of copyright material used in this book. The author and the publisher will be grateful for any omission brought to their notice for acknowledgment in the future editions of the book.

First Published 2013
Reprinted 2015

Viva Books Private Limited

- 4737/23, Ansari Road, Daryaganj, New Delhi 110 002
  Tel. 42242200, 23258325, 23283121, Email: vivadelhi@vivagroupindia.net
- 76, Service Industries, Shirvane, Sector 1, Nerul, Navi Mumbai 400 706
  Tel. 27721273, 27721274, Email: vivamumbai@vivagroupindia.net
- Megh Towers, Old No. 307, New No. 165, Poonamallee High Road, Maduravoyal
  Chennai - 600 095 E-mail: vivachennai@vivagroupindia.net, Tel. 23780991, 23780992
- B-103, Jindal Towers, 21/1A/3 Darga Road, Kolkata 700 017
  Tel. 22816713, Email: vivakolkata@vivagroupindia.net
- 7, GF, Sovereign Park Aptts., 56-58, K. R. Road, Basavanagudi, Bengaluru 560 004
  Tel. 26607409, Email: vivabangalore@vivagroupindia.net
- 101-102, Moghal Marc Apartments, 3-4-637 to 641, Narayanguda,
  Hyderabad 500 029
  Tel. 27564481, Email: vivahyderabad@vivagroupindia.net
- First Floor, Beevi Towers, SRM Road, Kaloor, Kochi 682 018
  Tel. 0484-2403055, 2403056, Email: vivakochi@vivagroupindia.net
- 232, GNB Road, Beside UCO Bank, Silpukhuri, Guwahati 781 003
  Tel. 0361-2666386, Email: vivaguwahati@vivagroupindia.net

www.vivagroupindia.com

ISBN: 978-81-309-2303-1

Published by Vinod Vasishtha for Viva Books Private Limited, 4737/23 Ansari Road, Daryaganj, New Delhi 110 002.

Printed & bound by Ritomate International, New Delhi.

M0000 / M0450

CONTENTS

ACKNOWLEDGEMENTS

Penning a book and spreading its pages to the public at large are in many ways like standing up in a gathering and sending out a personal voice for others to listen. I had always thought of this as an authentic mode of human living.

For enabling me to do it, I am immensely thankful:

To the several stalwarts in the field of Human Resources in Steel Authority of India Ltd (SAIL) especially to the guiding seniors Shri G Upadhaya and Shri G Ojha, for supporting me to experiment in the field of HR Technology.

To friends and colleagues in the HR Department including S/Sri HR Choudhury, RK Sharma, SPS Jaggi and Sri Anurag Nagar whom I regard as functional experts in different fields of Human Resources.

To present and past colleagues in the HRMS section of Bhilai Steel Plant: Sri PP Varma, BVN Prasad, Tushar Roychoudhury, MD Reddy, Venkatesh Kumar, P Sudhakar, RK Singh and my former office colleague Ms Rajeela Kumar.

To former executives and collaborators in C&IT department including Sri BS Singh and P Ajay Babu for collaborating and bridging the gap between knowing and doing in HRMS.

To system experts and programming resources in Research and Development Centre for Iron and Steel in Ranchi, especially to Shri Ashok Singh and Dr Usha Rani for providing me the first taste of technology in HR.

To my wife Jeeta and kids Harsh and Kanishka for sustained support in the general run of life.

And to my colleague Ms Aparna Chandra who did the tedious proofreading and corrections in the manuscript.

FOREWORD

I consider it an honour to write the foreword of this book. There are two compelling reasons for this privilege. First is the fact that I started my career together with the author in a remote iron ore mine, learning to learn on how to deal with people issues. Second is the fact that I always admired the objectivity and fairness of Nirmalendu in dealing with people issues, which is the foundation of HR.

There are three main arguments that this book contains:

1. It is not enough that HR be only a curious onlooker to developments triggered by IT; HR need to assimilate the core of it.
2. The above leads to the principle that HR should be aware of cultural implications of what the modern technology is creating.
3. Know your employees and understand them better with the aid of IT.

I consider this book as a sociological and historical perspective on the evolution of human resource management and how IT is likely to impact the way we work and relate at the workplace of tomorrow. It captures the evolution of the human resource function from the statutory upholder to the role of cultural modernizer of today in a very compelling manner.

Information Technology has transformed our lives in every way and the HR function is no exception. It has enabled automation of all transactional processes and eliminated human intervention through workflows. This has helped in one time entries and elimination of duplication of data entry in different HR processes. All organizations are enabling self-service through employee kiosks, desktops and laptops. Managers are provided access to all basic information, which enables them to be more effective and efficient. The book while providing hands on tips to design and develop inhouse HR database, urges the HR practitioner to use the IT tool to develop a technological temperament, and know the employees progressively.

The book lucidly illustrates a practical approach to application of information technology to human resource function to improve employee and employer productivity.

The only word of caution would be to remember that all technologies including information technology cannot substitute face-to-face interaction with the employee and hence HR professionals should continue to enable and build on human relationships within and outside the organization.

S Ramesh Shankar

Executive Vice President &

Head Human resources

South Asia

Siemens

Chapter 1

TRADITION AND MODERNITY

1.1 Words as Codes of Our Existence

1.2 Amazing Predominance of IT on Our Culture As It Works More on Our Mental Categories than on Physical Abilities

1.3 Modernization Is Vital to HR Function

1.4 Lack of Modernization Is Also Making HR Impoverished

1.5 Signs of New Generation HR Problems

1.6 Closeness to IT Will Enable the HR Functionary to Know the Employees Better

1.7 And How This Book Unfolds Itself

1.1 Words as Codes of Our Existence

If the reader is asked to pause a moment and list down the words that come to mind about modern life, the list with marginal variations from person to person would most probably run like this:

Windows
Fundamentalism
Help menu
Glitz
Network
Dot com
E-commerce
Cloning
Underworld
Mobile
ERP
PIN
Terrorism
Email
Corruption
FAQ
Files
Swineflu
Terror
Transaction
VAT
Privacy
Paperless
Open
BOT
Knowledge
Innovation

Overload
Improvization
3G
Community
Sustainability
Climate
Carbon
Compatibility
Context
SMS
Online
Code

You can continue to write the list longer.... and longer; but at any point of time an outstanding number of them would pertain to Information Technology. The brightest and loudest of words will also pertain to Information Technology.

Words that spontaneously float in our mind are like our existential codes. Like the genetic codes, these strings of spontaneous words will be unique to each of and or their common denomination would be unique to the time we are living.

Predominance of IT related words in our mind and daily life is the evidence of the cultural orientation today. Our work, personal and local life is flooded with concepts and products of information technology. This new technology has created cracks in most of our classical paradigms surrounding concepts of time, space, volume, limits, reality, facts and fiction.

The entire modern civilization can now be perceived as a logical arrangement of bytes of information. About a decade back and even now computer programming is considered as an esoteric activity. It looked exoteric from outside. If you come close to it, it would look as simpler as this:

(program to increment salary annually)

Declare the proposed increase in salary as a percentage.
Begin doing the following
Do the following till all are covered
Increase their salary by declared percentage
If the person is an underperformer
Don't increase
End of action for meeting above if
End of list of action for all people
End of the program

1.2 Amazing Predominance of IT on Our Culture As It Works More on Our Mental Categories than on Physical Abilities

The word information technology is now a way of normal life. But sometimes you will also feel its strong cultural shocks. For instance, fully computerized office processes are now available to us at many public places; most commonly in a railway booking counter, or a personal banking centre. Next time you walk into such a place, you only have to compare with earlier times and experience the difference. In the old classical office, the executive is located in a separate chamber implying hierarchy and the decisions can not be taken without his seal and signature. He symbolizes the centralization of reality in that office and remaining people are mere appendages. There is hierarchy. In your current window, watch how in the IT enabled office, there is no hierarchy, jobs are decentralized. There is a good probability that you and your work would have nothing to do with the executive, leave apart his seal and signature.

In the manual office, the official activities are either personalized or callous. You have to talk to many office people: clerks, cashier, and accountant. Talking to them make you realize they are either empathetic to your need or indifferent to the same. In the current window, you do not except a personalized interaction. This is more so as it is the computer which is at the helm of affairs most times and not the operator.

As your request was under process in a traditional office, each and every milestone was visible. Progress in the job would be slow and lingering. You can tediously watch your case inching towards the end result. There would be a perceptible sequence of events as your paper moves from desk to desk and you all through carry an ambivalence of jobs getting done and not getting completed. In the current office, the job execution is invisible as there would be no observable sequence of events.

Again as you walked into the classical office, you will mostly feel you are an outsider and carrying a lower status than the officials there. In the current situation, usually you wont feel any status perception vis-a-vis office staff as it is not him/her but the computer which is in charge.

Analyses in the classical office are man-made and there would be a uncertainty in your mind about the outcome at each stage. Activities can be repetitive in every clerical table that your file travels and multiple human agents may be scrutinizing your case again and again. Because of repetitiveness and human agency, decisions on similar cases can be contradictory. But not so in the current office. The system checks your case once for all and you do not expect a contradiction. There would not be any ad hoc decision as there are no changing interpretations.

In the classical office, your job gets distributed to number of tasks spread out physically at multiple points. The job is thus heavily dependent on a series of persons at different stages unlike in the new office. Your contact point is any one location, or the main computer there.

As evident from the above, most significant changes that IT has brought in, relate to our mental categories, our culture and not merely to our physical abilities and thus whatever works on intellect and culture, cannot be alien to HRM.

1.3 Modernization Is Vital to HR Function

A few steps back in history, the human studies officially known as HRM goes back to the days of Industrial Revolution when threats of human exploitation and problems of productivity were to be answered. Having answered these problems to a good extent, we the practising HR managers, have taken upon ourselves the task of cultural modernization and of the alignment of organizational culture with business performance.

These rampant issues are important and their tones are accentuating as the modern life is accumulating more and more computing and communication resources.

Opinions abound that bulk of the new millennium problems will not be technological but the expanding complexity of what it means to be human. Modern and successful organizations do spend a lot of time and energy on people issues.

Paradoxically, while assuming the role of a cultural modernizer, we ceased to be modern as a discipline in practise, for some time in the past. Even a casual observer will notice the growing signs of conservatism in HRM in practice. As a discipline we have perhaps not retained a live connectivity with the new ethos of the culture.

1.4 Lack of Modernization Is Also Making HR Impoverished

Clichés and dogmas abound in the HRM discipline now. Books and office plaques at many places have changed their titles from 'Personnel Management' to 'HRM' without changing any thing in substance.

Talking about innovation, hardly any new terminology of substance has been added to its vocabulary during the last two decades. Institutions and conferences have been mushrooming, but themes taken up and discussed have not changed in any significant way. As an HR Manager, when I compare my field with those of technical disciplines and functions like Finance and Materials Management, I feel we have not coped with the standard rate of progress and innovation around us.

This book is however not an admiration of information technology. It is about whether the technology and its world-view have given birth to a new kind of human type for us and has led to a new kind of culture. This book is also about a need to revise the basic assumptions of the way people live and work, more specifically work and production in industrial organizations.

While the number of men and women in the larger society and workplace who actually work on computers is still a small minority, its world view i.e. looking at human beings basically as receivers, processors and communicators of information is slowly submerging the current society. From metabolism of life with work or machines, we all have been moving to metabolism of life with information. The book is a promise to the readers to provide glance at the transition before the civilization is drowned by the new personality type.

Our subject of people management deals with an elusive object called employee; but, its elusiveness has been generally taken as counter scientific. For example, what are the main theories of HRM which will attract wide varieties of responses from practitioners? We have not been able to maintain a fair degree of standardization. Most other management disciplines are all visibly interconnected whereas our connectivity with other disciplines is absent.

In our daily lingo, we talk about HR as a non-technical discipline. This non-technical tag has kept us distanced from being scientific and modern.

Shri MN Shrinivasan an eminent sociologist of the sixties coined a word called *sanskritization* which can be mentioned to the readers here. After an intensive research on the *Coorgs* of

Mysore, he discovered that in order to raise their social position in caste hierarachy, the lower caste people undergoing economic progress started adopting customs and rituals of higher casts and gave up some of their own, considered impure by the higher castes. Later on he found similar patterns in many case studies elsewhere. He termed the process as *sanskritization* which was basically a cultural mobility to new rituals and practices when economic progress reached them. This process has nothing to do with true modernization. Is the HR profession undergoing a similar process now, when a new technological movement has swept the world, swept all other management disciplines or has it struck to its traditional tools?

1.5 Signs of New Generation HR Problems

Lack of cultural modernization has been creating many problems in our discipline. The lessons of history indicate that when cultural change does not keep pace with technological change, it leads to many tragic times. The last technology centered cultural changes occurred during the Industrial Revolution. As one enters into the information age, we must work in such a way that the painful features of the Industrial Revolution do not get repeated. What are these painful features of the Industrial Revolution? Well a lot has been written about them both by historians and by some of the great novelists. In *Oliver Twist*, Charles Dickens mixes grim realism with merciless satire to describe the effects of industrialism on the 19th-century England. Oliver, an innocent child, is trapped in a world where his only alternatives seem to be the workhouse, den of thieves, a prison sentence, or an early grave. From this unpromising industrial/institutional setting, however, a fairy tale also emerges. In the midst of corruption and degradation, the essentially passive Oliver remains pure-hearted; he refrains from evil when those around him succumb to it.

Let us now take the case of a call centre which is perhaps the most rapidly growing labour market sector today. Call centres are relatively new organizational units that use telephony and computers to manage communication with customers, the public, or government agencies. The conditions at work place are stressful, the working characterizes high mental load and constant attention, often coupled with irregular working hours. The work at the call centre is often performed 24 hours a day, all days during the week. You could therefore suppose that a part of the problems are about stress and its effects and the effects of the working time on recovery and sleep. These are some of the signs of lack of alignment between HR interventions and technology change.

The book will escort the readers to a new universe, where human entities behave so differently now. In the traditional paradigm, the individual in organization was an independent and unitary entity, moving in a fixed organizational space, with a fixed set of relationship mainly based on historical information. Most of the existing HR systems are based on such a concept of man. The new individual in contrast is now 'connected' to other individuals on a vast bed of information; the work relationships are 'dynamic'; individual actions change things simultaneously in 'multiple spaces' based on real time information. The book will also try to empirically project that this inadequacy is reflected in current human problems in industrial organizations

Are we trying to exaggerate the relationship between technology and human theory? I think its not so. Technology has always been the base on which human theory grew as a superstructure because of the unbroken and continuous reciprocity between doing and thinking. Human action immediately changes the objects and their properties, and so creates for our probing eyes, mind and grappling hands a new mental framework.

Apart from the cultural link what bridges both the disciplines together is that both deal with infinite and the dynamic elements and therefore closeness to IT will also enable us in knowing the employee better.

1.6 Closeness to IT Will Enable the HR Functionary to Know the Employees Better

Information technology apart from being the nucleus of contemporary culture, also has great potential for effectively handling the HR function assignments in industry situations as listed below:

- Long term HR plans with perspectives on how the human elements of the organization will shape over a period of time.
- Annual Planning and budgeting the human capital.
- Rightsizing and considering the implications of volume of workforce.
- Approach for separation of employees including early separations.
- Organizational structure and the hierarchy in which jobs are distributed within the organization.
- Merger of human elements of two organizations into one new organization.
- HR productivity or measures to improve output per worker.
- Scanning human implications when a major change is introduced.
- Redeployment and retraining or developing an employee in a new job location.
- Succession Plans or finding a new person within the organization to take over when an old employee separates.
- Ways to store, retrieve and disseminate employee knowledge.

- Benchmarking activities in which we systematically compare with other organizations having best practices
- Periodic audit of human institutions within the organization.
- Recruitment planning and schedule.
- Methods adopted for selection of new members to the organization.
- Fixing of wages for the employees, Pay for performance.
- Benefits-in-kind to the employees.
- Employee welfare.
- Process of measuring performance of employees.
- Controls on human behaviour through disciplinary activities.
- Ensuring provisions as per law of the land.
- Administrative trivia.
- Ways and means to address grievances.
- Identification of gaps in the competencies of the employee and arranging trainings.
- Long term IR perspective to cope with the collective power of employee associations.
- Employee communication.
- Climate survey and employee satisfaction feedback.
- Creating an environment where people will tend to learn and develop themselves.
- Counselling of the deviant behaviour.
- Human Motivation.
- Induction or assimilating a new member in the work culture.

Having introduced the problem, let us spread the road map that the book follows. 'Information Technology' and its devices, symbolizes what is modern today. Human studies are part of the traditional disciplines, but continue as a core area of concern even today to most of us, from profit planning business managers to spiritualists and novelists. The book attempts to project the need for a fundamental nexus between the two disciplines. The nexus is needed as the HR discipline must follow a route of cultural modernization. The modernization process needs to be visualized in the following way:

1. The behaviour of human actors in an organization has no independent self-subsistence as it is in constant dialogue with extensive changes happening in the outer socio-economic field. Our approach should enable us to grasp history and biography together i.e. the broader developments going on in the outer society and the personalized changes happening in the life of the individual in the industry, and their inter-relationships. That should be the promise of HR.
2. What is the structure of this particular society as a whole? What are its fundamental components, and how are they related to one another? Where does this society stand in the historical development of civilization? What is the meaning of any particular feature within it for its continuance and for its change?
3. What are the mechanics by which the behaviour of human actors in industry is changing? What is its place within and its meaning for the development of work culture as a whole?
4. How does any particular characteristic of technology and culture we are examining affect, and how is it affected by, the historical period in which it moves?
5. What varieties of human being now operate in this society and in this period? And what varieties are coming to prevail? In what ways are they selected and formed, liberated and repressed, made sensitive and blunted? What kinds of 'human nature' are revealed in the conduct and character we observe in the society in this period? And what is the meaning for 'human

nature' of each and every feature of the society we are examining?

6. The reasoning to all above can be based on the coincidence of dissimilar things and observing the interrelationships; structure with function at macro level as well as local level, the small and big milieu, the individual, diad, team and higher structures and finally the changes originating internally and externally.

1.7 And How This Book Unfolds Itself

The next chapter (Chapter-2) deals with human entity as a subject matter of study. It makes an ontological analysis of man, highlighting his ecstasy, dynamism, uniqueness and self-relatedness. While accepting that a full-fledged measurement of human being is not possible, it hints at how a scientific database on human factors can help in qualitative improvement in HR decisions. More importantly, it highlights the practical relevance of IT paradigm in reorienting HR perspectives, a paradigm which aims at measuring everything and bares the anatomy of IT hardware and software, and details the logical pattern which the mind in computer programming follows.

The subsequent chapter (Chapter-3) elaborates on the perspective of cultural modernization in a society dominated by IT.

Chapters 4 and 5 speak about human processes involved at the conceptualizing and designing stage of HRMS mainly focusing on practical experience.

Chapter-6 provides the concluding notes.

Chapter 2

DIFFERENCES AND SIMILARITIES IN HRM AND IT

Four types of differences:

2.1 Freedom of Action in Human Actors Contrasts Rigid Technological Procedures

2.2 Constant Tendency to Go Beyond the Present Status, Makes People a Different Entity Every Now and Then.

2.3 Every Person Has a Uniqueness of Being and Hence Prevents Any Comprehensive Classification or Generalization Needed for a Scientific Database.

2.4 Tendency to Examine All Actions to One's Inner Self Makes Human Being an Unpredictable Entity.

Four types of similarities:

2.5 Both Disciplines Encounter Subjects Which Have Infinite Parameters

2.6 Both HRM and IT Deal with the Human Intellect

2.7 Both Are Oriented to Handle Large Volume of Change

2.8 Both Subjects Are Marked by a Process of Convergence or Unification of Dissimilar Features

2.9 Human Side of Codd's Rules

Four types of differences:

The immeasurability of man in workplace is perhaps the most prominent difference between the two disciplines of HRM and IT as it is apparently a kind of obsession with information technology to measure everything, then store and finally process.

In fact there are four types of dissimilarities between the two disciplines:

- Freedom of action in human actors contrasts rigid technological procedures
- Constant tendency to go beyond present status in man makes him a different entity every now and then
- Every person has a uniqueness of being and hence prevents any comprehensive classification or generalization needed for a scientific database.
- Tendency to align all actions to one's inner self makes human being an unpredictable entity.

It is one of the self-evident facts of life for us, HR practitioners, that there are hardly any generic solutions for human events. Where the same incentive scheme will motivate one group of employees in one department, it will become defunct in another. The same Industrial Relations strategy will satisfy one group of employees but would irritate another group. Human issues are far more connected than we sometimes perceive and each entity has his uniqueness. Measurements are latest trends in all most all fields of management including HR. But then, we all are aware about limits and scope of measurement in human affairs.

There are many features in human nature that establish that human elements will always elude measurement.

2.1 Freedom of Action in Human Actors Contrasts Rigid Technological Procedures

Freedom of action is one of the fundamental nature of human being. We are used to a popular interpretation of the term of freedom in a negative manner and measure it with the absence of any physical restriction or being away from any kind of control. But then freedom is not merely what is demonstrated in such physical facts. Freedom is in fact primordial and exists much before the consciousness about the presence/absence of limitations. It sums up to initiating a choice, to arrive at decisions and provides a basic dignity to human action. There is probably no demonstrative way of proving the primacy of freedom conditions in human life, but all of us know beyond reasonable doubt that most of the tragic experiences of life and work life are rooted in the ever going tension between the pursuit for freedom and the limitations imposed by the life in a rational organization.

2.2 Constant Tendency to Go Beyond the Present Status Makes People a Different Entity Every Now and Then.

Human beings are ecstatic. The word ecstasy here does not carry the religious sentimentalist connotation which is normally attributed to it. Instead it implies the dynamic character of human life. Where most other types of entities in this world exist in the sense they may just be lying around, man is known to be continuously emerging out from its existing status to an ever changing new being. We all have a constant tendency to go beyond our existing status to what we think as better levels. This dynamic tendency in human beings makes it almost impossible to ascertain his exact nature.

2.3 Every Person Has a Uniqueness of Being and Hence Prevents Any Comprehensive Classification or Generalization Needed for a Scientific Database.

No individual is 'replaceable' or 'interchangeable'. 'Mr X' or 'Mr Y' is not specimen of a class; each of them is an assertion of a separate existence. Of course, if we take the concept in a little physical sense, no two objects in this world are identical. For instance, two copies of the same book may have slight difference in size or letter type here and there. However, the point of deliberation here is that such differences are superficial. It is a matter of great indifference which of the copies of the book I pick up and read and having read that I need not read thousand other copies in the market. But the same thing perhaps can not be said about the human beings each of which has a fundamentally unique existence. We fall into a fallacious trap when we surrender to statistically processed data, assuming that each person is somewhat like a manufactured thing with fixed and standard properties.

2.4 Tendency to Examine All Actions to One's Inner Self Makes Human Being an Unpredictable Entity.

Either man is living authentically or falsely. The difference in these two kinds of living is explained by the fact that either man is going beyond his current status to a more developed status or he is not himself and is being absorbed into the world of objects as just another inanimate object. The overwhelmingly complex pattern of human existence oscillates between man who is in line with himself and one who has deviated from his true self and may probably be acting to the detriment of himself. Unlike robots, we intermittently get into introspective mood and always relate and review our actions with our inner mind.

From the above, it is clear that a person can not really be measured nor can the data be totally be collected for storage. Inspite of all these philosophical handicaps, management specialists have been working tirelessly on HR measurements. HRMS packages developed all over the world are also constantly working more and more on human affairs in organizations.

Four types of similarities:

There are four types of similarities in IT and HRM:

- Both specialize on subjects which have infinite parameters.
- Both deal with mental categories.
- Both disciplines are oriented to handle complex changes.
- Both subjects are marked by a process of convergence.

If you introspect a little deeper you will find there are many parallels between human studies and information technology. In our view, these similarities demand more serious relationships between both the disciplines.

2.5 Both Disciplines Encounter Subjects Which Have Infinite Parameters

One prominent reason is that both deal with infinite properties of entities. Each human entity is a sum total of infinite characteristics which are in turn connected to several physical and psychological factors. Same with information technology; as days pass the storing capacity and active memory and processing capacity are touching infinity. Let us for a moment think about several fields of HR where such extraordinary large volume of data can help:

- Millions of data in thousands of fields regarding employee can be stored, retrieved and a picture of his total person will be available for taking a wholesome decision.

- Greater analytical ability will be available for more informed HR planning.
- Thousands of managerial, behavioural and technical competencies can be identified, and qualitatively better training need can be evolved.
- Performance management can be improved as you can maintain several details on tasks assigned, there can even be a daily measurement of performance.

2.6 Both HRM and IT Deal with the Human Intellect

Next to infinity, is the fact that both information technology and HR deal with the human mind; both of them work on upgrading intellect and mental capacity of the human mind. We, HR managers, need to appreciate this potential of IT. The progress of human civilization till date has been due to improvements in tools and equipments which leveraged the physical abilities of the man be it a wheel, an axe, steam or electricity. As Bill Gates has mentioned in his best seller book *The Road Ahead,* compared to improvements in physical abilities, IT enables an improvement in the intellect.

2.7 Both Are Oriented to Handle Large Volume of Changes

Both deal with a very complex onslaught of changes happening to its subjects of interest. Automatic updating of data by capturing every minute change in reality is one of the core principles of computer system. HRM also deals with human entities that internally keep on generating change and tracking and addressing significant changes in human conditions is one of its core responsibilities.

2.8 Both Subjects Are Marked by a Process of Convergence or Unification of Dissimalar Features

Last but not the least is the phenomenon of convergence; the coming together of two or more disparate disciplines or technologies. For example, the fax revolution was produced by a convergence of telecommunications technology, optical scanning technology, and printing technology. Our cell phones are now a convergence of telephony, camera as well as a music player. This is the cultural beauty of IT: of combining dissimilar objects at one point. The convergence phenomena in IT are similar to HR issues where different subsystems work to produce the deliverables. For example, human motivation is a combined output of the salary system, rewards and recognition, job content and work culture. Competency of people are decided by their practical knowledge, skills and attitude.

The information technology is now available to us in a wide spectrum of channels. From the smooth office packages, there are complex arena of multimedia, gaming, communication and entertainment. But for any of us in HR field, most vital to understand is the principles of RDBMS (Relational Data Base Management System). The RDBMS is the domain in IT which focuses on systematic storing and actively considering a very large pool of data. It should attract the attention of the entire HR community as an area which will remove our handicap as to how little we know about our employees when we take so many vital decisions which affect him. The practising HR manager however needs to learn a little bit of logical pattern which some of the packages on database including its latest version known as RDBMS and related programming languages follow, even if he doesn't have to participate in day to day programming. An RDBMS presents the data to the users as relations (It stores in a tabular form, i.e. as a collection of tables with each table consisting of a set of rows and columns). It also provides relational operators to manipulate the data in tabular form. E. F. Codd, a pioneer thinker of the mid-eighties, set forth thirteen principles which ideally an RDBMS should follow. To appreciate the potential of a RDBMS, HR practitioners need to appreciate these rules.

2.9 Human Side of Codd's Rules

Codd produced these rules as part of a personal campaign to prevent his vision of the relational database being diluted, as database vendors scrambled in the early 1980s to repackage existing products with a relational veneer.

The Codd's rules are as follows:

Rule 0 : For a system to qualify as a relational database management system (RDBMS), the system must qualify as relational, as a database, and as a management system. That system must use its relational facilities (exclusively) to manage the database.

Rule 1 : The information rule: All information in the database is to be represented in one and only one way, namely by values in column positions within rows of tables.

Rule 2 : The guaranteed access rule: All data must be accessible by means of primary keys. It says that every individual scalar value in the database must be logically addressable by specifying the name of the containing table, the name of the containing column and the primary key value of the containing row.

Rule 3 : Systematic treatment of null values: The DBMS must allow each field to remain null (or empty). Specifically, it must support a representation of "missing information and inapplicable information" that is systematic, distinct from all regular values (for example, "distinct from zero or any other number", in the case of numeric values), and independent of data type. It is also implied that such representations must be manipulated by the DBMS in a systematic way.

Rule 4 : Active online catalog based on the relational model: The system must support an online, inline, relational catalog that is accessible to authorized users by means of their regular query language.

Rule 5 : The comprehensive data sublanguage rule: The system must support at least one relational language that has a linear syntax, can be used both interactively and within application programs, supports data definition operations, data manipulation operations, security and integrity constraints, and transaction management operations.

Rule 6 : The view updating rule: All views that are theoretically updatable must be updatable by the system.

Rule 7 : High-level insert, update, and delete: This rule states that insert, update, and delete operations should be supported for any retrievable set rather than just for a single row in a single table.

Rule 8 : Physical data independence: Changes to the physical level (how the data is stored, whether in arrays or linked lists etc.) must not require a change to an application based on the structure.

Rule 9 : Logical data independence: Changes to the tables, columns, rows, and so on must not require a change to an application based on the structure.

Rule 10 : Integrity independence: Integrity constraints must be specified separately from application programs and stored in the catalog. It must be possible to change such constraints as and when appropriate, without unnecessarily affecting existing applications.

Rule 11 : Distribution independence: The distribution of portions of the database to various locations should be invisible to users of the database.

Rule 12 : The nonsubversion rule: If the system provides a low-level (record-at-a-time) interface, then that interface cannot be used to subvert the system, for example, bypassing a relational security or integrity constraint.

The complex nature of man maps well with the complexity of Codd's rules. For example, with reference to rule 0, HRM deals with employees as individual, diad, team, family as well as organizational entities. Similarly as regards rule 1, employees are identified as unique individuals and like to be acknowledged so. With reference to rule 2, HR interventions need to be more and more individualistic catering to the employees' unique needs. The fact that no RDBMS fulfills all the rules reminds us about how human behaviour does not fit into any set of logical principles. The complexity of human emotions befits Codd's rules.

Chapter 3

PERSPECTIVES OF HR MODERNIZATION

3.20 Organization Goal

3.21 Job Design

3.22 Training and Learning

3.1 The Cultural Impact, and Knowing a Person Better

In the previous chapter, we learnt about the similarities and differences between HRM and IT. We found how man is not perfectly measurable and also that how Information Technology cannot work without measuring the entities. Why then are we looking for a meeting ground for these apparently contradictory fields? Because we also find there are many significant points of similarity. These similarities enable very interesting meeting points between the two disciplines. Exploring these meeting points, one can discover how IT has ushered in a new culture and how IT would enable you to know your employees better.

We deal with the culture impact in this chapter and about knowing the employee better in later chapters.

The hypotheses in this chapter are based on research work involving primary and secondary data on a large manufacturing facility with reference to three stages i.e. 1960-80 (stage-1), 1980-2000 (stage-2) and the current century (stage-3). The milieu refers to a large manufacturing unit in Public Sector in Central India.

The typical human being is now increasingly found to be an information processor from the role of a producer of goods and services. This itself is a fundamental shift in cultural values, behaviour pattern and activity. Unlike many animal species, most human knowledge of how to act is learned rather than genetically built-in. In complex societies, individuals do not carry all necessary information in their brains. Instead, they rely on the external storage of information in the form of culture. Culture is a broad term defining the entire way of life shared by a people. While it includes our tools and artifacts, much of human culture consists of information. Language, ideas, beliefs about the meaning of life, and information representing our shared impressions of the physical world are all part of our culture. In practical mode, culture consists of three components: Value (defined as 'what is important in life'), Behaviour (denoting 'what kind of behavioural pattern would result in achieving the values'), Activity ('what kind of activity helps in attaining the values').

Oxford Advanced Learner's dictionary of Current English defines technology as "study, mastery and utilization of manufacturing and industrial methods; systematic application of knowledge to practical tasks in industry". Technology i.e. the methods and tools by which man handles the forces of nature, has been the prime mover of all human developments in all stages of history. The economic, social and cultural patterns in a community are built accordingly. But there is also a constant dialogue between technology and culture. If technology affects the culture, culture also affects the technology.

History follows the course of man's mastery of the external environment in order to satisfy his needs, at first the basic needs of food and shelter, but later broadening into higher level needs of culture. Thoughtful leaders in the past have established co-relation between different stages of technology and development of human culture; between hunting and tribal culture of Stone Age, between agriculture and slave society, between the stagnation of dark ages and feudalism, industrial revolution and capitalism and now information technology with the post-capitalistic society.

The pre-historic ages like Palaeolithic times, were marked by virtual absence of technology or rudimentary techniques of what is termed as stone technology. With the advent of metals like iron and bronze, the agricultural society emerged. Slavery and feudalism were significant marks of the society and culture in these days. With the introduction of better naval technology, mercantilism as form of socio-economic system followed. The eighteenth century industrial revolution saw a spate of breakthrough inventions rapidly followed by emergence of factories, and the spread of capitalism and imperialism. The post-industrial society and economy in the twentieth century were marked by continued scientific inventions in wider areas including electronics, nuclear and the information technology contributing to the modern cultural values.

Since tools and artifacts are an important mark of culture, it is relevant to list down the major tools which the modern man uses today worldwide over:

- Networking by which several numbers of computers and human users share a wide variety of information on real time basis.
- Search engines which enables an user to find relevant information from a sea of data in Internet.
- Email which facilitates transmitting of information from one user to another any where in the globe and irrespective of the fact whether the user is logged into computer or not.
- General purpose PCs which can handle words, numbers, data, pictures, sound and mailing.
- E-Business which facilitates commercial transactions through net.
- ERP (Enterprise Resource Planning) by which the organization may contain many departments and functions but on computer they behave verified and facilitate quick response time.
- Multimedia by which apart from data, sound and pictures are also available to the user.
- Video conferencing where people can talk through computer with visual impact.
- Mobile communication where you can send and receive information wherever you may be.
- Convergence implying merging of various technologies which are traditionally thought to be different from each other like electronics, telecommunication, entertainment etc.

- Paperlessness by which computer enables storing of large volume of information and records without the traditional medium of paper.
- Computer-aided design (CAD) can be described as a partnership in which the computer quickly performs the drudgery and the person provides the creativity.

We have already discussed that there is one major difference between impacts of computer as compared to other technological innovations in the past. The computer as a technology is an upgrader of human mind while all earlier technology have basically enhanced his physical power.

Computer has become the symbol of modernity in the last quarter of the twentieth century so much so that the period has been termed as information age. Computer technology in practical terms represents the introduction of new tools for communication, information processing, and remote control. Technology, however, is more than about tools. It involves the social processes, behaviour and cultural values in producing and using tools. The cultural relevance of computer is immense and to be explored from academic point of view. It is also useful for social planners and organizational administrators to understand the implications before introducing computer based changes.

For practising HR managers, cultural changes can be perceived at two domains; the domain of local society with its unique community setup, and the domain of a formal business organization which is the main economic basis of the local community.

In the context of social domain, the following major sub-elements have been dealt with:

3.2 Components of Social Domain

Social space : Social space denotes pattern of social action towards persons placed at various degree of distances.

Sense of time : Time, like space is another fundamental dimension of the physical world and changes here are significant for our cultural frameworks.

Social Action : Manner in which two or more people communicate and modify one another's actions.

Typical personality : Every age and every culture gives rise to a typical personality type as a generic framework of cultural activities.

Social Groups : Groups of various types operate in the society. The primary groups are close knit, informal, small in size and based on daily interactions like the family and work teams. There are then the professional associations and organizations which are secondary and based on voluntary membership.

Family : Family is the most important primary group in the society.

Differentiation, stratification, cooperation and social conflict : These are various substructures and processes in the fabrics of society which social scientists study in order to arrive at their functionality.

Communication : Forms of communication, points to communicate and tools of communication are important cultural marks of a given society, and more so in the modern context.

Language : Language and Literature are important cultural dimensions of verbal and written communication in any society.

Socialization : Socialization is the process in which the individual imbibes the social norms of his community.

Leisure : Activities in which individuals engage themselves in leisure hours are very significant from the point of view of cultural analysis.

Religion : Religious practices are very significant as it influences the values and behaviour of people.

3.3 Components of Modern Organizations

For analytical purposes, the following elements of organization have been studied in this paper:

Goals : Organization goals implying both the long term vision, mission, strategies as well as short term targets.

Organization Structure : Organization structure reflects the size, shape and distribution of powers and roles among various groups.

Reference Groups : Among various groups, reference groups are those who hold a higher status and other groups try to emulate them.

Job design : Job design reveals the nature of work assigned to workers and managers.

Recruitment and Induction : denote the methods of granting new membership to the organization as well as facilitating the new to imbibe the values of the organization.

Training and Learning systems : indicators of development environment in the organization.

Performance Appraisal : methodology by which work is measured in the organization and subsequently linked to the system of reward. Salary, rewards and quality of work life are also culturally relevant as they affect the performance behavior of the employees.

We must be aware that we have entered into the atmosphere of another age. All of us should be aware of the spectrum of cultural changes that is passing through our time both in the larger society as well as in the organizational life. While we are generally alert about the changes in human behaviour in the organizational set up, we need also to be aware of changes in behaviour in the outer society which sooner or later affect the organizational behaviour too.

3.4 The Arena

Bhilai was one sleepy and unknown village in Central India which provided space for a mega steel plant constructed as a result of the philosophy of government, to make public sector steel plants as infrastructure to extensive industrialization. The Union Cabinet approved the Bhilai Steel Project the location of this study as an Indo Soviet collaboration on 27th January 1955. The Plant began its operation on 31st January 1959 when Coke Oven Battery No.1 was commissioned. The Blast Furnace No. 1 was inaugurated with production of pig iron on 4th February 1959. Steel making began on 12th October 1959 in the open hearth furnace No.1. Rolling of steel started on 12 November 1959 subsequently the last of the six open hearth furnaces has been commissioned on 22nd February 1961 marking the completion of the one million tonne steel project.

Considered as a work horse by steel industry watchers, the plant has undergone two expansions there after. The first expansion work began in August 1962 and could be completed by the middle of June 1967 when it achieved the production capacity of 2.5 million tones of crude steel. The second expansion project was initiated in 1975. The second expansion was a major technological achievement in terms of indigenous project management. Lots of indigenous equipments were also used though the quantity of foreign equipments used was as high as 87%. This expansion is also important in the history of Bhilai as the plant went for production of flat products: the heavy plates.

Today, the plant is certified to all the four international standards of ISO-9001 : 2000, SA 8000, OHSAS 18001, ISO 14001 and has a turnover of over Rs. 18,000 crores with a manpower of 31,000 distributed in 110 production and service departments. The Plant has an immaculate track record of continuous profitability for last two decades. BSP also bagged the prestigious Prime Minister's Award as the best managed steel plant in the country in public and private sectors, nine times during the last sixteen occasions from the points of view of production, profitability and employee productivity and work culture.

From the large technological grandeur that the plant projects, let us have a look at its organizational climate.

3.5 The Human Development

Organizations, like we individuals, live and grow with a unique personality of their own which distinguishes them from the others. This uniqueness is rooted in a complex blend of values, traditions, conventions etc. The members of the organization work within and are continuously influenced by this internal environment, which is called organizational climate.

Organizational climate, therefore, is characterized by the following:

a. Description of the uniqueness of the organization.
b. The quality of the internal environment as perceived by the members.
c. Elements that influence the behaviour of the members i.e. facilitate or constrain human resource activities.

Based on a climate survey, the average man in this organization is:

- generally satisfied with his job
- feels that scope for enhancement of knowledge and skill is available to him
- fairly clear about his role
- is also substantially open to his superiors and colleagues. May be due to this, he perceives a strong helping relationship within his primary work group

- but then similar openness is absent while encountering higher management. In addition, matching degree of help has not been coming from outer groups
- he has adequate faith in his colleagues, but suffers from loss of confidence at macro level
- he enjoys good deal of freedom of action, but has reservations about supervisors and interferences in work-in-process
- he takes pride in identifying with the organization when he is meeting outsiders, but inwardly unsure whether personal loyalty or organizational loyalty is paramount. He therefore does not feel dependable about the official channels of communication
- in the depth of it, he may be skeptical about whether he is living up to his true self

3.6 Space in Which We Live and Operate

Space and time are mind's categories ever since days of Immanuel Kant and have always conditioned our worldview. They are two fundamental parameters of our encountering the physical world; of our value system, and influence our pattern of behaviour as well. All of us would recall that a couple of decades back, living in the society was like the concept of space in Classical Physics, denoted by a fixed point implying specificity, limitation, definite and permanent boundaries. Individual could exist and act at only one point of space at any given time. One of the traditional features of space is the sense of distance and the limitations created by it. In the industrial organizations which came up in the fifties, when large scale Public Sector based industries came up in the country, hundreds of people from various parts of the country would arrive at the locations for employment, would get recruited; but then the fear of distance from their home place will make them run back to where they belonged.

There are records that people will repeatedly run away to their home town, absenting for months, sometimes as long as an year and then the financial compulsions will bring them back to the manufacturing site. The tendency changed dramatically as we advanced through time. Better communication in terms of transport as well as telecommunication helped in modernization and people became comfortable in being in frequent touch with outer world.

Also in the real space, if an individual is at one point, he/she cannot exist in another point at the same moment of time. There are evidences that people including the executives would work at one place in their entire career and would love to be in that one location all through. Transfer from one department to another was rare and many times was taken as a kind of punishment. As time passed, and service functions like marketing, finance became more important globally, people tried to move over to these functions.

The traditional properties of space have been strongly challenged by information technology. In client server technology for example, one is causing changes at one's PC terminal and simultaneously is also changing things at the server end which stores the data. The traditional mind will be amazed to watch how we are impacting on two places at the same moment. A report software run at a remote terminal would trigger a 100 page print action in a line printer several miles away. Sometimes this gives a feeling that I am here and I am also elsewhere at the same time, and thus culturally attacking the traditional notion of being fixated at a single location. The feeling accentuates when you work in a large network say net applications where your action could be changing things at several points physically located at great distances. All these lead to a value system which thinks that the classical reality with its limits of space is not enough; it projects the legitimacy for 'virtual' reality also.

Absence of a sense of distance, frequent mobility and multi-locational existence are the new cultural traits in people and employees triggered by the information technology.

3.7 Our Sense of Time

Let us now be aware as to how our orientation of time has changed as we have walked into a world submerged by information technology. Upto the seventies in organizations, there was a visible dependence on the past. The method was historical. Present is only a child of the past. For example, last year we performed at the rate of 'x' so this year we must make it to a few percentages more.

The on-line culture makes available the enormous data about the present as it is happening. Let us the compare this with how traditionally we have been depending on the historical method in all our approaches; the method based on data of the past. Some years back, whenever there was a problem in the factory site, we looked for how the same problem was solved in the past. The production planning and control departments' annual report continues to prominently reflect the past record in all the performance factors. The organizations of the eighties saw a spate of long term planning activities. It became really fashionable to have 'future' projections on all functions of industrial activity as we were moving closer to the epochal year 2000 AD. There would be 7 year, 5 year and 3 year plans on almost all areas apart from annual budgets and monthly targets. Here the 'future' replaces 'past' in our value system. High priority is attached to the concepts like growth, progress and acceleration. The tomorrow is going to be definitely better. This could be because of the utopia effect of Y2K, the epic year of 2000. For ages, the year had meant end of most of the human problems.

Come back to the 'now', currently the reality is amazingly under our control and we can intervene in the 'present' process as soon as it is taking shape. A shift to 'Present' is the most important dimension of our time today. Information Technology can now capture the present effectively which was not the case earlier. Its no more an elusive reality. We are in synchrony with the present and can intervene and act as the things actually happen. The emphasis on past, future and present respectively comes out as marks of the three phases of our industrial culture in 1950-70, 1970-00 and the twenty-first century.

Another complimentary process where technology affects our perspective of time can also be mentioned here. Earlier, people worked at a pace set by machinery and enforced by supervisors. While the logic of factory machinery required a temporal discipline on the part of workers, in new computer systems the machine can accommodate multiple tasks occurring at different tempos, in different sequences and in flexi-time. The new technologies can be used to coordinate work performed by individuals acting at their own paces and under their own directions.

3.8 Social Action

A particularistic social relationship is one which is based on emotional evaluations of who a person is. Race, sex, kinship and other characteristics acquired at birth are used to determine how to act towards another person. Clear distinctions are made between behaviour appropriate towards strangers and behaviour appropriate to one's own primary group. Universalistic social relationships are based on general principles for acting towards other human beings. Rational judgments of how a person is acting are more important than who he or she is. The modern culture shifted from particularistic social relationships into universalistic ones. The positive contribution of universalism to human interaction was a greater willingness to cooperate with people outside one's own family, locality, or region. The negative aspect of universalism has been a loss of social solidarity in family and community, and a lack of consensus in values. There has been a clear movement of culture to this direction.

Individual consciousness was initially 'tradition' directed in line with the culture of dependence on past. In the second phase, individual is 'inner' directed as he becomes introspective and goes for self-analysis about his own strengths and weakness. With the interventions from information technology, the individual has acquired a character of 'outward' directedness as he searches for best solutions all over the world and not necessarily in his neighbourhood or within himself.

3.9 Typical Individual and His Personality

Every era with its unique technology gives rise to a typical man. It is important to mentally draw his profile before we deal with him.

Individual in the first stage was living under strong 'community' forces. In our reference case, since the work for new projects gave similar type of jobs to them, there was a kind of mechanical solidarity among them. All of them existed because they worked for the erection of those structures. This was the first phase where the individual lived under strong community forces. There were restrains on the individual mainly arising out of both tradition and organizational procedures.

With the passage of time in phase-2, the environment became fiercely individualistic as pressure on performance and quality increased.

In the present phase, the tendency to remain connected to everybody and ready availability of information on every thing make people closer to world of work. Informal and formal matrix organization and exponential change in communication mechanisms have made the individual connected to a larger group of people.

Individual now increasingly gets 'connected' to a larger community. Man gets his meaning from how he relates to so many as he turns into a 'being-with-others'. But how friendly can a computer or cell phone be, when "friend" is a social relationship? Are you talking more to computers and less to people? For some thinkers, the dilemma of modern humanity has been the development of instrumental rationality in science, technology, and business at the expense of the human need for meaning, continuity and belonging derived from direct, face-to-face interaction with one's particular group. The advantage of the rationalization of culture has been the development of universalistic social relationships. We are able to form larger communities and treat strangers with less suspicion. The disadvantages have been individual isolation, reification of social relationships, and a weakening of shared norms and values. Computer-based communication shows evidence of being a continuation of the trend towards universalism in social interaction. It also offers some new possibilities for enhancing social integration in organizations and communities. Like in outer society, life within work organization is a highly connected one. My reflective self in this world of work tries to define itself by relating continuously to many others, many roles in various departments.

Life now gets meaning from its connectivity to several others in this world and we want to be continuously in touch with them. Life also seeks meaning from large volume of data collected from all possible sources. The tendency to generate and process data is very evident from the forms of new appraisal systems, formatted manner in which human processes were cast in Standard Operating Procedures, and visible linkages between various management strategies like the linkage between long term plan, short term plan, Internal Customer Satisfaction Plan, departmental Plan and individual KPAs. The individualistic man is gradually fading away or left behind and giving way to a new man, who is unendingly connected to data lines.

3.10 Groups in the Society

Sociologists have defined groups as aggregates of individuals in which definite relations exist between the individuals comprising it and each individual is conscious of the group activities. Social groups are classified as primary and secondary. Primary groups are defined as 'intimate, emotional, private, face to face and exclusive living together exemplified in family, kin groups, neighbourhood in a village and group of friends. Secondary groups in contrast are infrequent associations of people, intellectual in character and normally of large sizes like a country, city, or a club.

Strong primary groups have all through been predominant in traditional life and these groups are formed based on kinship, nativity and language basis in earlier times. As we move forward in industrialization, the power of work teams will gradually over take the influence of the community and language based groups. Predominance of religious organizations gradually changes and individuals are dominantly influenced by primary groups at work place like department, section and brigade. Departments were exclusive groups having a unique function like coke making for Coke Ovens and iron making in Blast Furnace. Sections were functional subdivisions within department. Like there would be operation, mechanical maintenance and electrical maintenance sections in all production shops.

Financing and credit organizations emerge in large numbers as man becomes individualistic and sense of growth and achievement overtake other concerns. Yet widely scattered people have been maintaining their social ties through letters, phone, and periodic gatherings. Some families plan annual reunion with dozens of aunts, uncles and cousins; there are caste and community based gatherings in regular periodicity. Professional institutions meet periodically for presenting papers and interacting with fellow professionals.

As we step into the current time, the secondary groups become visibly more powerful than the primary groups and this is facilitated by the technological ability to interact with larger groups even if they are physically far away. Secondary groups also become more differentiated, specialized and some times involve short term relationships. There has been immense differentiation also in the nature of secondary groups. These groups now take up specialized areas. Association with these groups is often temporary. Once a person learns a new computer course, he leaves and thereafter contacts are feeble. Also a person becomes member of several numbers of groups that may include religious, educational, entrepreneurial and sports. The preference attached to secondary groups like professional bodies also indicate a choice to remain connected to the outside world. In work place, Power, impact and effectiveness of physical work groups are relatively declining. Easy and effective communication mechanism is making it possible that individuals team up with the best partners not necessary the immediately available partner to form the work teams.

3.11 Family and Kinship

The family is an institution, not found in its totality in any pre-human species. The family was made desirable by the need of prolonged child care along with the need for hunting with weapons over large terrains. The family has certain economic, and reproductive functions. Joint family was the order in the pre-industrial age. In fact, in every period in history, there is a tendency in the predominant form of technology or economy either to form a joint family or a nuclear family. Agriculture and trading business mostly favour joint families, which need a large well knit group. The industrial economy similarly needs nuclear families, which can be mobile and which can subsist in places far away from native locations. Nuclear families came up as people flocked for employment in the greenfield sites.

A surprise development after entry of information technology is that the nature of family becomes independent of the technology unlike earlier times. This relationship between technology and family has now perhaps become very weak. Because of increased communication avenues the nuclear family has now acquired the advantage of joint family and vice versa.

Firstly, the extensive availability of telephony and thereafter the availability of inexpensive personal computers with internet, enabled people to shop, obtain information, transact business, and communicate with others without even leaving the home. Home computers represent a new form of social integration, reconnecting the separation of work and personal life that occurred during the Industrial Revolution. Alvin Toffler argued that personal computers will make work at home more common, giving us "electronic cottages". Even if home computers do put work and family life in the same place, it is highly unlikely that large corporations will distribute their considerable economic power to new home-based industries. Those who view the electronic cottage as a return to the good old days before the Industrial Revolution when families were economic units, may be having an idealized view of traditional families and of modern economies. Whatever the directions in home computing, it seems unlikely that they will in themselves relieve the interpersonal tensions to which the family is subject.

3.12 Process of Cooperation and Differentiation

The manners in which people gather together to cooperate in carrying out certain category of activities and the way they engage in conflict, are marks of their culture.

Initially, there was a very marginal differentiation. But status differences were very rigid between groups like executives, supervisors and workers. The differentiation was quite rigid leaving almost no scope for mobility from one group to another. Cooperation was mainly based on nativity and language. The level of cooperation thereafter shifted to primary work groups. Now there is a very high degree of differentiation. Cooperation efforts are more in secondary groups and combine dissimilar functions like it happens in the technological 'convergence'.

In the first phase, we find very little cooperation except at the work place. The additional cooperation areas were limited to community or religion based activities. Specialised areas of cooperation were added as time passed. There were practices in shop floor having cooperative financing and close group blood banks. These additional cooperation was still very dependent on fundamental groups like work groups, departmental groups or religious affiliations. In contrast, now individuals quickly gather to handle time bound projects and disperse after some time when the project gets completed. This is true for both work as well as the outer society.

Computers would tend to be viewed by functionalists as a technology that increases the adaptive capacity of a society by enhancing its ability to gather information about the world and to make vital decisions about itself and its environment. It tends to connect more to macro society rather than micro society.

3.13 Information and Communication

Initially it was practically a less communicative society in the greenfield site of the case manufacturing unit. Whatever information people received at the construction site was through official notifications or through the post. In the initial days, even newspapers were not available. Two Hindi dailies of "Hindustan" and "Nav bharat" made appearances in the early sixties and a house journal was published from 1961. In the next three decades, number of newspapers published multiplied, though quality of information may be varying. Also number of captive/official telephone connections multiplied from a few hundred to 5000 in this period. Only the business communities in the region, banks and institutions had the P&T telephone connection.

The tools of communication have since changed in power and quality. Telephone booths mushroomed throughout the region. The number of in-house official telephones increased to 10,000. Data transfer through computer networks was gradually implemented. Towards the end of the period, mobile phones had made entry, rapidly bringing in a culture of accessing information as the event takes place. While these tools were instrumental in communication process in secondary groups, the primary groups were holding departmental communication forum which facilitated structured face to face communication within the group. But even then the face to face component of communication was getting into the declining trend. Almost every house has now a telephone and many with internet connection.

What is most important in face-to-face contact is our ability to imagine ourselves in the presence of another self. Because this is an emotional response to another person, the addition of non-verbal elements can make it easier to perceive another's humanity. The negative effects of computer-based communication, loss of face-to-face contact, strains on trust, and a reduction in normative social control are balanced by the possibilities for social integration in communities formed around electronic networks.

Communication, especially mobile communication is practically a continuous activity. This communication activity is not necessarily based on a pre-planned need but happens as a natural on-going life process almost like breathing and thinking. A point to be thought about is that, are we transforming ourselves from a thinking and feeling entity to something busy in collecting and transmitting information?

3.14 Socialization

Through socialization, individuals acquire the information and techniques needed to function in society, while society maintains its culture and social structure from generation to generation. Socialization teaches people their roles and places in consonance with established norms. It provides them with norms of behaviour, values to live by, and beliefs to explain how and why they "fit" in a society. The family and the school are the two most important socializing institutions; for within them, children are introduced to the intricacies of their culture. For older children and for adults, social networks and economic institutions are important agents of socialization, providing opportunities to learn new social roles and behaviours.

Earlier days in the case manufacturing site, socialization was a slow and lingering process due to poor availability of information and slow rate of learning. Emphasis on socialization later on was laid as the organization puts high value to maintain its work culture. Socialization is soon becoming non-issue as involvement is task oriented, learning is in high scale and information is quickly available. The adults now enter various associations and voluntary groups as fast as they exit. Their involvement is task oriented and therefore social cohesion is not required from the source of tradition. Also earlier learning was slow because it needed time and energy to have information about the community, which is not the case now.

3.15 Recreation and Leisure

Leisure is usually thought of as "free" time during which we voluntarily choose an enjoyable activity. Computers as tools for work and as toys for play obscure the relationships between work and leisure. 'WORK HARD, PLAY HARD' says an advertisement for a standard computer brand. We tend to think of work as time spent on activities we are paid for. Initially, unplanned and unstructured leisure and sometimes no leisure hours existed as people cope with tough industrial life and there used to be heavy pressure for project completion. In the second phase, leisure is planned and arranged with infrastructural support from the organization.

Management in construction sites has from the beginning been participating actively in providing leisure activities and recreation to the local community. Community centres have been constructed and financial supports have been provided by the plant for various sports and games as well as other cultural activities. Radio and film shows were very popular recreation modes at this stage. The cable TV, video cassette libraries were added in the nineties. Towards the close of the nineties, electronic, computer games and cybercafes joined the stage and became very popular. The small township has now as many as fifty cyber cafes. Video games, which may appear as simply another expensive fad, are seen by some analysts as part of a new pattern of life. Children learn about social expectations through play, and can often be found "practising" grown up roles.

Computers also obscure the divide between work and play. Social psychologists worry that video games reduce children's opportunities to engage in social interactions. While the characteristics of computer games which allow players to interact quickly with complex arrangements of information certainly introduce children to the human/computer interface, the crucial issue is the degree to which computerized recreation distances human players from experiencing physical and social interactions. In the entire development however, recreation and entertainment are also getting highly individualized and the need for physical gathering of people like in a movie hall or a theater show is gradually reducing.

3.16 Religion

In the small town we have been referring, establishment of religious shrines mushroomed one after the another in the first phase. Religious considerations are in a high scale as individuals struggle for stability of life in a radically new kind of situation, an industrial set-up and become wary of their anonymity, isolation and finitude. Achievement oriented activities during the eighties and the nineties put religious activities in a low scale. Revival of religious consciousness has recently been flourishing among the new age youngsters. Religious value is a psychological disposition which connects the finite individual with the infinite entity. The revival matches with the tendency of self to remain connected with global super-self. Many new spiritual school based communities flourished in all ranks of the community.

In religious or mystical experiences people report a self that is part of the whole universe. If your sentences described your relationship to the sacred, you were describing this dimension of self concept. Because the computer interface can heighten our feelings of connectedness and our feelings of power, it is possible that the technology will encourage such a self concept. Attachment to religion has not dwindled at all with the radical changes in culture. Attendances in many religious institutions have in fact been increasing. This is rather surprising as there exists a common myth that modernization increases rational thinking, hence distancing from spiritualism.

3.17 Change Producing Behaviour

Change has traditionally been like an interruption on normal life. Changes poured into the sleepy villages by the external agents of modernization and industrialization. Intermittent expansion of the plant, mushrooming of ancillary and small scale industries around the main project site provided further impetus to the modernization process. In the subsequent period, most change interventions were indigenously forged by way of self analysis and introspection.

Subsequently, a wide range of changes both extraneous and indigenous, were adopted after making a systematic measurement of the organization culture and climate survey. The modern phase is marked by all round changes in quick succession. Now it looks like a continuous field of ever changing form; change in pattern reverberates all around. These interventions are indigenous interventions like attempt to measure HRD orientation in the organization, structured step by step interventions to manage absenteeism, weekly forum where chief executive of a 50,000 workforce meets the public visitors on Sunday mornings, an interaction forum where the Training department holds a session with the newly recruited trainees and their guardians, new recruitment categories for job-enriched positions, counselling services including a laboratory where the section head and union officials jointly hold a session with deviant employees etc. Combined with this was also an equal series of external interventions like Internal Customer Satisfaction (ICS) model for qualitative improvement of annual plans, TQP and ISO 9001 quality system in works, and HR. Changes flooded so comprehensively and so continuously that it stopped looking like interventions any more. Universe looks like a vast field of ever changing forms.

Organizational Life

Human Resource System in business organizations have undergone radical changes in last three decades. These changes are generally presented as shift from 'Personnel' function to HRD function. Let us have a look at these changes.

3.18 Organization Structure

There is a constant dialogue between culture and structure in every society as well as in each organization.

Organization structure traditionally is an instrument which controls the main channels of flow of activity and authority in the organization and in concrete terms visible in the form of size, shape, groupings and hierarchy. The organization structures were earlier very elaborate and rigid and were very religiously followed. The organization chart could run onto eight levels corresponding to eight grades of pay. There were notified delegation of power for every level of hierarchy. Decision-making processes in files more often than not specified who should take the decision.

Later on, it was felt that there is a need to prune the structure and reduce the layers in the organization chart so as to facilitate quicker decisions. A consultant appointed during this period suggested that there should be maximum two levels below the head of plant operations. The dialogue between need for reduced levels and hierarchical traditions continued well up to the mid-nineties, but the organization structure did not undergo any radical change.

Recently, it is noticed increasingly that such experimental structures of hierarchy are still being prepared but in practice are soon forgotten. There have been two instances where redesigning of organization chart was thought to be a solution to speed of decision making and organization wide exercises were initiated. But finally the activities died down. On the other hand many successful projects are completed due to better horizontal coordination among different functional groups without a proper notified organization structure. Delegation of power was almost a forgotten document except for certain major financial decisions and statutory activities.

In the making of the HRMS in the case organization, group of officers and staff from several departments like EDP, Personnel, Finance, Time Keeping were involved. The R&D organization which conceptualized the major plank of the system had ofcourse signed a formal agreement with the steel plant. But in retrospect, the actual process and area covered were more often at variance with the original plan and more attuned to the growing needs of the HR function.

But the most glaring example about activities in contrast to notified organization structure is perhaps the implementation of integrated HR-Payroll technology. There were many processes where both HR and Finance were involved. For example when an employee was promoted, promotion decision is taken in HR department, his increase in salary is also decided in HR department. HR issued an administrative order which was sent to Finance carrying the promotion decision and revised salary of the employee. The Finance used to recheck the calculations, feed the data into their Payroll system and on the salary day used to send the advice to the employee's bank. With the introduction of the HRMS, it was felt that Finance as an intermediary may not be necessary as the calculation in HRMS is done by the computer. Also re-feeding the data at Finance end into Payroll system has the potential for error in feeding. Appreciating that there is no value addition in the process at Finance end, the Payroll was directly connected to HRMS and so when HR decided the promotion the revised salary automatically updated the Payroll. Apart from efficiency in terms of time and accuracy, the system also made free the entire group of Finance department who were full time engaged in verification and data feeding.

The main channels of activity is decided by agreed purposes, individuals and projects. The intensity of activity is more at team level than at hierarchy level. Also the pattern of interaction will soon be changing as the project assignment is over. Normally a person should be in discomfort on these fast changing relationships, but its not so in real.

3.19 Reference Group

Supervisors and groups engaged in hard production shops in the steel plant were reference groups earlier. Initially, the supervisory position known as the chargeman was the main reference group. The worker always chased the dream to become a chargeman even at the fag end of his career. Similarly, workers engaged in core iron making and steel making units were considered a reference group with high value attached to the hard work and arduous working conditions amidst heat and dust.

In contrast, persons working in computer are now being placed in a higher status in the formal and informal organization. There are many evidences on this. Employment CVs carry prominently skills on computer. Every department, one or two persons who actually manage the PCs for MIS are viewed with admiration and jealousy and many times attached to the offices of HOD. During the inception of HRMS, there was a flood of requests from officers and staff to get posted to the section.

All the above go to establish the fact that the computer educated has truly become a reference group.

3.20 Organization Goal

Commissioning and continuous growth in production were the goals during the inception of the plant. Goals lacked proper focus. A steel plant has been established and therefore we have to produce steel as per the technological capacity. And to grow, we have to produce, let us say a few percent more in quantity and quality in every passing years.

In the intervening period, full capacity production, technological and administrative discipline became points of emphasis. Goals were set with more detailed formal procedure after the introduction of the methodology of brainstorming among board level members and the organization wide learning of these goals. In the pre-liberalization era, the focus of corporate change was people. In the post liberalization period, the customer and his market are drivers of change. It is however people who continue to make change happen internally. They must however be constantly in touch with the outer world and be prepared to face the external challenges with their collective power. All the people awakening exercises arising during the period have attempted to carry home this message.

In contrast during the current phase, new goals are re-examined in fast frequency involving lot of accumulation and processing of data. The organizations in the current phase defined their goals in cultural terms like core values which give a sense of dynamism and liveliness than the earlier goals of physical outputs. Change, Corporate Strategies, Customer Satisfaction, Internal Customer Satisfaction, Benchmarking, Global Competitiveness, Accelerating the Pace of Change, Transformation etc. are the key words used during and after the director's workshop.

For the student of human studies, it may be relevant to look into the fact that all the goal setting and goal clarification process are simultaneously a process of creation and augmentation of what can be called 'information capital'. The workshops were preceded by large scale empirical research and also followed by ground level information gathering before implementation.

3.21 Job Design

Job design initially was on skill base and evaluation of a set of linked factors. Actual working hours were of non-standard nature. Overtime was prevalent abundantly throughout the period. Jobs were designed and ranked as per evaluation on thirteen parameters including educational requirement, experience, initiative, skill, responsibility and environment. The work required mostly a single skill and involved mostly carrying out the executive decisions for certain kind of output. There were practically no defined working hours under the pressure of completion of projects at various stages of the commissioning of the units and under the arrangement of overtime.

From single skill, there was a gradual transition to multi-skilling in the mid-eighties. In the early eighties the sixty thousand plus pool of direct manpower were distributed into 134 departments, 360 sections and 3200 designations. With the downsizing prospects ahead, there was a need to come out of the limitations of compartmentalized jobs. Also man-hour utilization in mono skilled jobs was very low. Therefore efforts for multi-skilling and merger were tried out during the late eighties.

As time passed, job designs have now become dynamic, open ended, cross functional and project based. Work got more strategically organized. Cross-functional responsibility got increased.

3.22 Training and Learning

In the initial days, development of employees focused on key steel making 'skills'. Technical Skill was considered as the entire gamut of competency which decides the effectiveness of individual at work place. It all started with skill because information on skill in the sixties was rarely available.

Systematic management education in collaboration with foreign consultants implied emphasis on 'knowledge' and 'leadership skills'. In the seventies and the eighties, there was a thrust on these two domains.

Behavioural and team building training with emphasis on employee 'attitude' entered in a visible mode in current time.

New contents of industrial training has been shifting from technical skill to behavioural human relation areas. This might be due to increased availability of information about management training and sensitivity training which was earlier available in major urban locations only. True that bulk activities still continue to be skill development, but new efforts in training have been clearly going into areas of quality, action orientation, planning methods, interpersonal behavioural training.

At this stage, it may be interesting to watch the correlation between above cultural changes as well as the widely discussed transition of traditional Personnel Function to the modern Human Resource department. Prof Udai Pareek and Prof TV Rao have identified the following shifts:

Personnel Function and Human Resource system : A Comparison

S. No	Personnel Function (PF)	Human Resource system (HRS)	Information Technology related culture
1	PF is an independent function.	HRS is a sub-system of a larger system (organization).	Real things are never standalone; they are always connected to a larger totality.

2	There are several sub-functions under PF.	HRS is an organic whole: all the parts are interlinked.	High degree of interlinkages between all segments.
3	The main task of PF is to respond effectively to the demands (coping role).	The main task of HRS is to develop enabling capabilities (proacting role).	Universe is a vast field of ever changing patterns and HRM should align with the same.
4	PF has the main responsibility for personnel matters.	All managers share the responsibility of human resource management.	The system encompasses all the nodal points in the organization.
5	The main responsibilities of PF relate to salary and job administration, and management of people and their development.	The responsibilities of HRS relate to people systems, and the process of the total organization.	HR should therefore undertake more informed decisions based on a large volume of live information.
6	The major attention of PF is on personnel administration or management.	The major attention of HRS is on developing people and their competencies.	Human competencies are always interacting with the cultural elements.

7	Personnel system and procedures should be designed to achieve maximum efficiency.	HR systems and procedures should be designed on the basis of process values to reduce human wastage.	Speed and accuracy must be accepted as values in the HR system.
8	People in an organization are motivated mainly by salary and rewards.	People are primarily motivated by challenges and opportunities for development and creativity.	Access to HR database can open up new avenues for development and creativity.

There is thus a clear indication than IT is building the new paradigm of culture.

Summarizing all that was happening in this chapter, let us have a snap shot at the imminent cultural changes which information technology has been causing to our culture:

1. Absence of a sense of distance in *space*, frequent mobility and multi-locational behaviour are the new cultural traits in people and employees triggered by information technology.
2. Control over the 'present' in *time* and liberation from timings decided by machinery.
3. In *social action*, the progressive culture is enabling transition from particularistic social relationships into universalistic ones.
4. Life now gets a meaning from its connectivity to several others in this world and the *typical Individual* and his personality want to be continuously in touch with them.

5. Currently, the *secondary groups* become more powerful than the *primary groups* and this is facilitated by the technological ability to interact with larger groups even if they are physically far away.
6. A surprise development after entry of information technology is that the nature of *family and kinship* becomes independent of the technology unlike earlier times. Because of increased communication avenues, the nuclear family has now acquired the advantage of joint family and vice versa.
7. *Differentiation* is becoming more elaborate and *Cooperation* efforts are happening more in secondary groups and hence combining dissimilar functions like in the technological 'convergence'.
8. *Information* and *Communication* activity is not necessarily based on a pre-planned need but happens as a natural on-going life process almost like breathing and thinking.
9. *Socialization* is soon becoming irrelevant and a non-issue as involvement is task oriented, learning is in high scale and information is quickly available.
10. *Recreation* and *Leisure* is becoming more and more individualized as a person doesn't need to be a part of a group of audience in the recreation facilities. Computers also obscure the divide between work and play.
11. Attachment to *religion* has not dwindled at all with the explosive changes in culture. Attendances in many religious institutions have in fact been increasing.
12. *Changes* flood us so comprehensively and so continuously that it stopped looking like interventions any more. Universe looks like a vast field of ever changing forms

13. The main channels of activity in organizations are decided by agreed purposes, individuals and projects in the team rather than the hierarchy of the *Organization structure.*
14. The computer educated have truly become a *reference group.*
15. *Organization goals* are re-examined in fast frequency involving lot of accumulation and processing of data.
16. *Job designs* became dynamic, open ended, cross functional and project based. Work got more strategically organized. Cross-functional responsibility increased.
17. *Behavioural and Team building training* with emphasis on employee 'attitude'.

Chapter 4

KNOWING THE EMPLOYEE BETTER: THE DESIGNING AND DEVELOPMENT PROCESS IN HRMS

4.18 Anybody Can Do the Work of a Specialist

4.19 No Need to Physically Send Any Report

4.20 Decision Support System: Breaking the Limit of Hierarchical Decision Making

4.21 Automatic Tracking: Events Announce Their Arrival by Themselves

4.22 Process Efficiency: Speed, Lesser Cycle Time

4.23 Accuracy , Automatic Updating

4.24 Convergence: Ensemble of Dissimilar Entities

4.25 Delegation

4.26 Generic Office System

4.27 Codification of Employee Data

4.28 The Data Entry Process

4.1 Capturing the Complete Employee

Why do we generally think that we will always take authentic decisions when dealing with our own friends? It is because we know them thoroughly. Across the years, as we have been interacting with our friends, we have been gathering piles of data about them and this data pool gives us the advantage to take a wholesome decision about them. We know what will make him happy and what would disappoint him. It is an accepted fact that we can take best decisions about a person if we know him adequately. For the practising human resource managers like us, many professional problems would stand resolved if there is a way of knowing the employees better.

Our profession deals with people elements who have near infinite numbers of properties. It is many times in number if we compare with the physical or chemical properties of an engineering product. Traditionally, there has been a handicap about collecting and storing such a large volume of information and that too about a large group of persons. There was also no way to collate and process such information to draw a complete picture of the man we are dealing with. The manager's handicap at this point is compounded by the fact that man's uniqueness and affinity for freedom makes him a dynamic combination of these properties.

The superlative degree to which computer can store volumes of information, and also the ease with which the same can be updated therefore should be practicably utilized by the HR managers to capture knowledge about the true person in employees. I feel one real and practical challenge for the IT as a discipline is to make this happen, and we in the HR field should also spend good deal of energy and action in this direction.

4.2 Re-engineering HR

IT's revolutionary effect on business has been powerfully brought out in the books of Robert Kaplan.

Let us list out some of these effects relevant to HR in the table below:

shared databases with networking	• consistency in data • live and real time participation • liberates from limit of sequencing • benefits of both centralization and decentralization
expert system	• a generalist can do the work of a specialist
decision support system	• tools to break the limit of hierarchical decision making
automatic tracking	• events announce their arrival by themselves
process efficiency	• speed • accuracy • automatic updating • lesser cycle time
convergence	• fusion

As we progress in this chapter, we will find how these properties of IT can lead us to some amazing solutions in HR field.

In the rest of this chapter we spend on how a process of knowing and serving the employee better was actually materialized in the process of designing a Human Resources Management System. For this, we may refer to the case *industrial organization* described in Chapter-3.

4.3 Taste of New Technology

It has been said that new technology many times appears first as a fad or fashion, thereafter as a need and finally as a dire necessity. This is true for the world of computers also.

In the mid-eighties, we in the HR group, had our first taste of computer when two Buroughs-25 machines of Tata-Burroughs make were procured. Some of us in the HR department persuaded our seniors and joined the one week training program conducted by M/s Tata-Burroughs. Computers were not yet the in thing in steel industry. But the week's classroom and hands on sessions were truly mesmerizing. The trainer took us to word processor first and explained to us step by step how it answered all the requirements of a writer. The spreadsheet looked as if stolen from the paper register and pasted on the computer monitor and was a big help in MIS areas. But what struck us like magic was the RDBMS (Relational Database Management System).

The RDBMS known as the 'data manager' was very powerful by those days' standards. The data manager made us realize that relationships between information are not only textual or mathematical, they can also be logical. RDBMS enables one to predefine a few assumptions about how different fields of data are related or how they can be extracted from the database. As a result, the same data can be viewed in many different ways depending on the need of each user. An important feature of relational systems is that a single database can be spread out across a network of several tables. This differs from flat-file databases, in which each database is self-contained in a single table.

Later on with the advent of multi-purpose PCs in several versions, the 'dBase' became very popular especially because of the beauty of its programming language. The spreadsheet was also used, but not very extensively. The word processor was ofcourse dearest to us as HR function in those days throve on extensive report writing work. Many of us learned the skill basically because of the excitement that the new concepts the word processor generated.

4.4 Encounter with a Multitasking Machine

Our faith on database was strengthened when in 1989 we procured another machine: HCL HORIZON-3. It was the first UNIX based system procured in our organization and had its own DBMS known as Unibase. We came to know that UNIX is important as it was the first Multitasking and Multi-user machine having the ability to execute more than one task from more than one user at the same time (a task being a program). In multitasking, the CPU switches from one program to another so quickly that it gives the appearance of executing all the programs at the same time.

Training and working on UNIX gave us the joy of brushing with something truly ultra modern. But because of disk space constraint in the systems those days, we could maintain the data of only 15% of total employees of our plant. The machine was thereafter basically used for MIS purposes.

For a full decade afterwards, we could do nothing more than toying with the idea of having a network of HR offices with a comprehensive computerized process. There were many reasons for this time lapse : the size and number of personnel offices, the exorbitant cost of computers in those days etc. When we put ourselves in top management position, it was indeed a difficulty to conceive investing a large amount of computer resources in the HR area where returns are never immediate. At the same time, two theoretical questions often troubled us in HR function. How can we take decisions about thousands of human beings without having adequate data about them? How can we aspire to be change agents of work culture while the most modern tool of science is not available to our profession?

In the next stage of development, we procured six PC-486 machines which were made part of a new section of computerization. This can be said to be the beginning point of a modern HRMS in the organization. It was decided to put 10 fields of vital information about each employee through these PCs in Oracle connected to a Sun server in EDP department and generate some basic reports like master list etc and a couple of MIS reports. Accordingly, the manual seniority lists were obtained from different departments one by one, and data were fed into developer forms.

4.5 A Collaboration Starts

As the data feeding jobs were in progress, RDCIS (Research and Development Centre for Iron and Steel), a sister unit of our holding company located at Ranchi, Jharkhand, offered us a project for computerization of a database with three to four connected PCs where we were promised that all employee services jobs like Leave and LTC can be handled. We were about to reject the offer as by that time we already started had the same job with the help of our in-house EDP department. But instead of rejecting the offer, we requested them whether they can help us in computerizing the activities in our widely spread out field HR offices; the offices which are our windows to the employees for various HR services. They agreed to review and after a couple of months showed us a glimpse of what can be done. We therefore signed a MOU of collaboration with them.

We then sat with the two dedicated programmers of RDCIS and started making the blueprint.

A computerization plan was drawn up with following objectives:

a. Extending benefits of computer to shop floor employees.

b. Making it comprehensive and to cover all areas of HR function, from recruitment to employee separation.
c. Upgrade the capacity of the HR department to store, analyze and support information about employees.

Looking ahead from this point, there were several aspects which looked utterly depressing:

- Management's normal hesitations for technological investments and hardware in administration functions.
- HR department is so much bound to traditions. We are so used to papers, cyclostyling, forwarding copies.
- Our officers were so unused to scientific activities.
- The size of human group is mammoth at 55,000 direct employees.
- We had heard about information network through telephone and modem but had never experienced it in reality.
- Personnel procedures and delegation of power were so complicated that we used to wonder whether any programmer would have time and aptitude to read through and transform them to electronic procedures.

4.6 A Day in the Life of an HR Executive

One of our approach was to reduce administrative trivia in our offices, so that the officers and staff can concentrate on finer aspects of HR.

We had asked our HR officers to log in data about different types of activities in which they are engaged throughout the day and also amount of type spent on them. The average pattern showed like as under:

- Fixing of wages for the employees.
- Pay for performance, incentives etc.
- Employee welfare.

- LTE (Local Travel Expenditure).
- Measuring performance of employees.
- Disciplinary activities to control human behaviour .
- Administrative activities like leave and LTC.
- Ways and means to address employee grievances.
- Identification of gaps in the competencies of the employee and arranging trainings.
- Industrial Relations interventions including long term perspective to cope with the collective power of employee associations.
- Perspective plan on how the human elements of the organization will shape over a period of time, matching with business requirements.
- Planning, budgeting and monitoring the pool of human resources.
- Recruitment, selection, induction and placement.
- Approach for separation of employees including early separations.
- Organizational structure or the way and hierarchy in which jobs are distributed in the organization.
- Merger of human elements of two or more groups into one new group.
- HR productivity or measures to improve output per worker.
- Scanning human implications when a major change is introduced.
- Redeployment, retraining and developing an employee in a new job location.
- Succession Plans or finding a new person within the organization to take over when an old employee separates.
- Ways to store, retrieve and disseminate employee knowledge and creativity.

- Benchmarking activities in which we compare systematically with other organizations having best HR practices.
- Periodic audit about human processes within the organization.
- Collective bargaining.
- Joint consultation.
- Participative decision making.
- Employee communication.
- Climate survey and employee engagement studies.
- Creating an environment where people will tend to learn and develop themselves.
- Counselling of the deviant behaviour.
- Human Motivation.

Groups of HR officers participated in a survey to skim out areas where the database, decision support and automation powers of computers can be truly beneficial to the profession. The survey instrument is shown at Annexure-1. From the same, we derived those which have ultimately been taken up for computerization.

The HRM areas where no significant contribution can be made by computers are where face to face interaction with the entities are a must, e.g., Counselling, Motivating or Industrial Relations.

The above enables a realistic analysis of need for computerization as shown in the flow chart given in the next page.

Flow Chart - 1

HRMS NEED ANALYSIS

HRMS business objectives

↓

Top management consent on the proposal

↓

Cross Functional team of IT and HR is formed

↓

Analysis of functions of HR offices and roles

↓

Survey on processes and activities in HR office and time spent

↓

Selection of processes for inclusion in HRMS

4.7 Preference for In-house Development of HRMS Database

We recommend in-house development of HRMS database better than buying an off–the–shelf product. Though it can not be generalized, large and complex organizations undergoing frequent changes in structure and HR policies should preferably go for in-house HRMS packages.

The software development is an enriching experience of partnership between the programmers and the functional specialists from the HR department. On the advice of our computer professionals, we decided to go for a client server architecture. This means there will be a main computer at the centre which takes care of safe upkeep of a central pool of data and a chain of smaller computers in different HR offices which takes care of their different requirements. Client server is network architecture in which each computer or process on the network is either a client or a server. Servers are powerful computers or processes dedicated to managing data and network traffic. Clients are PCs or workstations on which users run applications. Clients rely on servers for resources such as files, devices, and even processing power.

4.8 Oracle Was Like a Divine Solution

The decision was also to use Oracle as the database software which is held to be robust and with powerful safety features. We were impressed by the news that Oracle fulfils maximum out of the 13 rules of Codd. At the client end, it was decided to use Developer 2000 also by Oracle which ensured most of the events based on clicks of mouse and spared the HR users from the painful struggle with the keyboard. Oracle also accommodated the security features of Delegation of Power, a terminology which is frequently used by HR executives defining which user can see what information and enter/change what. For a mind which was used to watching data on the sheets of paper, it have been really tough to imagine the paperlessness in which the RDBMS kept its records. It took us several days to absorb the concept until I played extensively with Dbase.

As you participate in designing of an HRMS, you will be flooded with many manuals and guidebooks. Some of the key words that practicing HR managers should know are as under:

Database : Databases keep similar information at one place, like employee number, name at one place so that we can use it any place with identical features. Databases classify, sort, screen and combine information in multiple ways without duplicating the data.

Tables : In Oracle, and for that matter in any RDBMS, information is maintained as a set of tables. Each table in turn comprises of fields and records which can be visualized as columns and rows. Fields/Columns are therefore the vertical part of the table and the record/rows are horizontal. The purpose of existence of fields and records are completely different. Records hold different kind of information about one item whereas the fields contain similar information regarding many items. It is very easy to sort, filter, add, average, find, combine and manipulate data in unlimited ways.

Values : Values are like cells in a tabular structure and contain information corresponding to a particular row and column. In RDBMS normally you have to define the values as to their data types (three major types can be character, numerical and date), their length (maximum and minimum) as well as null or not null.

Relationships : Tables in Oracle database are linked through logical relationships.

Users and Roles : Every user is given an identity and a password which enables him to acquire the rights and privileges of a role.

4.9 Tables for HR Database

We started with about 60 tables covering various aspects of people management, which over a period of time has doubled. The typical ones are as under:

Table name	Brief description
AREAS	indicating broad areas of working like works, administration, mines

DEPTS	description and codes of departments
DEPENDENTS	list of various types of dependents, relationships with the employee, their age and status
DESG_CODES	complex codes of designations and its linkage to skill level, section and department
EMPLOYEE	core information about employee against the primary field of employee number
EMP_QUAL	list of qualification, codes and typology against employee number
GRADES	grades and different incremental amounts
GRADES_OLD	history of scales of pay from time to time
MEDICAL	events of treatments in company hospital and referral outside
PUNISHMENT	current disciplinary actions
PUNISH_DETL	detailed information about recent disciplinary actions
PUNISH_HIST	past disciplinary actions
RESTORE_DISCP	conditions like date by which pre-punishment status will be restored.
REWARD/ AWARD	appreciations, reward events and type of reward
ROSTER_POINTS	points to be filled up for specially reserved categories like SC or ST.
RELIEF_FUND	recording consent of employees to donate for relief in case of calamities
MULTI_SKILL	existing skill, additional skill in which he should be developed

SKILL_MAST	codification of skills and link with department
SKILL_TRG_DET	status of multi skill training
REDEPLOY	event where employee is redeployed from one job to another
SPOUSE	details of spouse if he/she is also employed in the company
POST_DEPT	posting department, other than the mother department
PROBATIONS	probation events, dates, decisions taken
REGULARIZATION	regularization information
SPL_PAYS	special components of pay which are personal to the employee
PAY_DATA	different components of pay against employee numbers
PAST_ EMPLOYMENTS	details of earlier employers and position held
PAST_ PUNISHMENT	disciplinary cases which have been closed
NOMINEES	dependents who have been nominated as beneficiary for various potential payments like PF , Gratuity etc.
NOM_GUARDIAN	details of guardians if the nominee is a minor.
PROM_HIST	past promotion events
APPRAISAL	appraisal grades assessed from year to year
LTC_DETAILS	leave travel details

LTC_CANCEL	cancellation information with regard to leave travel
LTC_PAYMENT	LTC payments advanced to employee ,and bill adjustments
EMP_LEAVE_ CREDIT	parameters of crediting Leave against particular type
LEAVE_DETAILS	accounts of leave availed
LEAVE_CODES	code and decode of various types of leave like casual leave, earned leave, medical leave etc.
INSTITUTE_CODE	codification of colleges and universities from where employee has acquired various qualifications
HRA_DETAILS	House Rent Allowances paid along with different parameters
HOUSE_MAINT	House maintenance amount paid to employee and its history
HELPSCREENS	long text descriptions and help codes
HEADS	Heads of Departments from time to time
FURNISHING_BILL	data on passing of furnishing expenses
FINAL_SETTLE	event details of final settlement once the employee separates
FESTIVAL_ADV	advances drawn during festivals
EMP_PASSWD	to store employees' password
LOAN_CODES	codes for various types of official loans
EMP_CATEGORIES	categories like physically handicapped or weaker section of society

EMERGENCY_CNTCT	details of whom to contact in case of any emergency like accident of the employee
GATEPASS	event details of issue of security passes to employee
DPC	event details of decisions of departmental promotion committee
DISCP_ACTION	current data and history of disciplinary action taken against different employee number
C_PATHS	path which regulates career growth and promotion of the employees
P_OFFICERS	details of personnel officers who function as users in different periods
DATE_BIRTH	specially for illiterate people who do not have a proper document on date of birth and various dates have been approximately mentioned in many secondary documents
PF_AMT	provident amount and dates of remission
COURT_CASES	data on various court cases where the employee has a role and its status
CONSENT	to store employee consent to various issues from time to time
CIRCULAR	circulars to be used in help menu
TRANSFERS	details of designation, section and department in internal transfers
BASICPAY_	changes in basic pay date wise across the career

BANK_CODES	codes of bank and branch where salary of the employee is to be credited
ATTENDANCE	details about number of days of attendance
ADDRESSES	permanent address for correspondence
QUAL_CODES	codes, description and hierarchy of qualifications
SECTIONS	section codes, description, department code where they exist
STERILIZATIONS	date and type of sterilization against employee number
STUDY_LEAVES	information on study leave
SUPPL_ATT	supplementary attendance of employees
SURETY_ DETAIL	information on employees who stand surety for other employees
TRADE_ TEST	dates, scores in test against employee number
TRANS_ ADDRESS	address of people after they are transferred to another unit
TRANS_ ATTENDANCE	attendance of employees who arrive on transfer from another unit
VEHICLE_DETAILS	registration details of vehicles owned against employee number
VEHICLE_LOANS	vehicle loan information
VEHICLE_LOAN_ OLD	status of earlier vehicle loan
VEH_LOAN_ CANCEL	cancellation event in vehicle loan process

VIGILANCE_MAST	list of live cases where vigilance investigation is going on
VRS_SETTLE	final settlement made after acceptance of voluntary retirement
ZONES	codes and descriptions of different zones in one area

Designing tables for every pool of information is a very specialized assignment for which one should consult the system analyst. The more planning one does at the time of table structure, better the productivity at the time of running of applications.

The tables logically contain columns (also known as fields) and rows. Data in columns are categorized into different data types Number, and type one self evident. The textual data are known as varchar type as per the database communications.

4.10 Columns in the Main Employee Table

The columns in the core employee master table for example would contain the following:

Fields in Employee Table

S.No	Fieldname	Type (Size)	meaning
1	PLNO	NUMBER (6)	employee number
2	CATEGORY _CODE	VARCHAR2 (5)	General, SC, ST etc

3	DESG_CODE	VARCHAR2(5)	multi-digit code which will describe the designation as well as indicate various characteristics of the post
4	GRADE	VARCHAR2(5)	code for scale of pay with increment amounts
5	DEPT_CODE	VARCHAR2(5)	code for the department
6	SECT_CODE	VARCHAR2(5)	code for sections within a department
7	DOB	DATE	date of birth
8	DOJ_COY	DATE	date of joining in the company
9	GOVERNING_ RULE	VARCHAR2(1)	code for service conditions by which the employee is governed
10	ACCOMO-DATION	VARCHAR2(1)	Y, if company accommodation provided
11	CL	NUMBER (3,1)	balance casual leave
12	DOJ_DEPT	DATE	date of joining in the existing department

13	HPL	NUMBER (3)	balance half pay leave
14	INCR_DATE	DATE	date of next increment
15	DESG_CHG_DATE	DATE	date on which current designation was allowed
16	RELIGION	VARCHAR2(1)	codes for religion
17	RETIRE_DATE	DATE	date of retirement auto calculated from date of birth
18	SEX	VARCHAR2(1)	code 'M' for male and like wise
19	DOJ_BSP	DATE	date of joining in the current plant/unit.
20	EL	NUMBER (3)	balance earned leave.
21	EMP_STATUS	VARCHAR2(2)	code to know the status of the employee whether currently working, transferred out, retired, resigned and so on

22	EMP_STATUS_ CHG_DATE	DATE	date on which the above status happened
23	EMP_TYPE	VARCHAR2(1)	codes for Regular employee, temporary or casual, trainee
24	EMP_NE_EXE	VARCHAR2(2)	code for executive or non-executive
25	FIRST_NAME	VARCHAR2 (30)	first name
	MID_NAME	VARCHAR2 (30)	middle name
26	LAST_NAME	VARCHAR2 (30)	surname
27	TITLE	VARCHAR2(3)	Mr, Mrs, Ms, Dr etc
28	BLOOD_ GROUP	VARCHAR2(5)	blood group
29	MARITAL_ STATUS	VARCHAR2(1)	marital status
30	FATHER_ NAME	VARCHAR2 (30)	name of employee's father
31	GRADE_DATE	DATE	date from which current grade is held

32	STERILISED	CHAR (1)	status of sterilization operation of the employee
33	ZONE_CODE	VARCHAR2(5)	code for the zone
34	AREA_CODE	VARCHAR2(5)	code for the area
35	PRESENT_ BASIC	NUMBER (5)	present basic pay
36	APPOINT_ TYPE	VARCHAR2(1)	recruited as what type: regular, casual or trainee
37	DPC_ SENIORITY	NUMBER (4)	seniority for the purpose of promotion
38	HARD_AREA_ TAG	VARCHAR2(1)	hard or easy job
39	HEAD-QUATER	VARCHAR2 (50)	city of posting
40	HOMETOWN	VARCHAR2 (50)	location as permanent address
41	MED_STATUS	VARCHAR2(1)	medical position
42	POST_DEPT_ CODE	VARCHAR2(5)	department if employee is posted in other than parent department

43	REMARKS	VARCHAR2 (50)	remarks
44	DA	NUMBER (7,2)	dearness Allowance
45	PF_LOAN_IND	VARCHAR2(1)	provident Fund loan indicator
46	FEST_ADV_IND	VARCHAR2(1)	indicator for festival advance
47	AUTO_ADV_IND	VARCHAR2(1)	indicator for auto advance
48	HBL_IND	VARCHAR2(1)	indicator for house building loan
49	HRA_IND	VARCHAR2(1)	indicator for House Rent Allowance
50	LEAVE_RULES	VARCHAR2(1)	category of rules deciding leave eligibility
51	BILL_NO	VARCHAR2(4)	bill number in Payroll
52	INC_CODE	VARCHAR2(4)	incentive code
53	DOJ_GRATY	DATE	reference date for calculation of gratuity

In Oracle, a user has a unique identity/name, a password and at least one role assignment. Roles determine the capabilities and privileges a user should have. The DBA can add and remove roles as per organization's requirement.

4.11 The Programming Language

There are several programming languages. But the basic pattern of their delivery style has not changed across the years. For HR managers who want to be associated as functional experts in HRMS designing, should be familiar with the nature of programs through which the RDBMS runs.

A program is an organized arrangement of instructions which when executed, causes the computer to behave in a predetermined manner. Without programs, computers are as good as dead. A program like a cooking recipe, contains a list of ingredients (called variables) and a list of directions (called statements) that tell the computer what to do with which variables. The variables can represent numeric data, text, or graphical images. There are many programming languages like C, C++, Pascal, BASIC, FORTRAN, COBOL, and LISP to name just a few. These are all high-level languages. One can also write programs in low-level languages called assembly languages, although that is more difficult. Eventually, every program must be translated into a machine language that the computer can understand. This translation is performed by compilers, interpreters, and assemblers.

4.12 SQL as an Example of a Language

HR managers using HRMS must have working knowledge about computer language specially SQL. SQL stands for Structured Query Language which lets you access and manipulate databases. SQL can execute queries against a database, retrieve data from a database, insert update records in a database, delete records from a database and create new databases. If the DBA so wants, it can also create new tables in a database, create stored procedures in a database, can create views in a database and also set permissions on tables, procedures, and views.

4.13 Developer as a Choice

An application is a computer program that does some task. A database application is a program that uses data from a database management system. Most database applications have to do with displaying data in useful ways or with entering and updating the data in the database. Database applications have their own requirements, interfaces, and languages, which make programming even more difficult. This is the reason why they provide application generators and report writers such as Oracle's Developers/2000 which make it much easier to develop applications. In their pure form, application generators are very powerful. With just a few statements or filled-in-fields in a form, one can generate very capable applications.

Modern applications generally consist of a graphical user interface with menus, toolbars, dialog boxes, and windows that display the application objects. The three kinds of objects of interest are as follows:

1. FORMS Applications (FORMS in application is like same as forms any where generating a place for user to fillup data)
2. REPORTS Applications (generating MIS)
3. GRAPHS Applications (Generating graphical MIS)

In Developer 2000, the HR person would be struck by two main themes, the GUI and the Triggers.

GUI expandable to Graphical User Interface is a program interface that takes advantage of the computer's graphics capabilities to make the program easier to use. Well-designed graphical user interfaces can free the user from learning complex command languages. On the other hand, many computer savvy users find that they work more effectively with a command-driven interface.

In an RDBMS, a trigger is an SQL procedure that initiates an action (i.e., fires an action) when an event (INSERT, DELETE or UPDATE) occurs. Since triggers are event-driven specialized procedures, they are stored in and managed by the DBMS. A trigger cannot be called or executed; the DBMS automatically fires the trigger as a result of a data modification to the associated table. Triggers are used to maintain the referential integrity of data by changing the data in a systematic fashion.

Each trigger is attached to a single, specified table in the database.

Triggers are hyper productive entities and can be viewed as similar to stored procedures in that both consist of procedural logic that is stored at the database level. Stored procedures, however, are not event-driven and are not attached to a specific table as triggers are. Stored procedures are explicitly executed by invoking a call to the procedure while triggers are implicitly executed. In addition, triggers can also execute stored procedures.

A trigger can also contain INSERT, UPDATE and DELETE logic within itself, so when the trigger is fired because of data modification it can also cause another data modification, thereby firing another trigger.

Flow Chart - 2

HRMS Structure

Selection of IT architecture

↓

Selection of RDBMS

↓

Selection of off the self/inhouse mode of development

↓

Selection of application/package

↓

Database design, tables

↓

Finalize Columns, Relationships in each table

↓

Users and Roles

↓

Codification (employee status, designation codes, Section codes etc)

↓

The technology of connectivity

↓

Installation of terminals

In designing the application, re-engineering plays a vital role. Examples are:

4.14 Single Application instead of Three Copies

Earlier employees may have to make multiple copies of application for any service they need in HR office. For example three copies are required to be stored as information, one with HR, another with Finance and a third with the employee for requests like LTC. Now you may decide to keep only one copy, may be only with the Finance for auditing. The other two, HR and employee can manage with access to the database when they need to check. Taking one step ahead would be areas where no application needs to be taken from employees.

4.15 Consistency in All Reports

Earlier, if the same data was asked to different agencies, it was possible that they would have given different figures. Some departments would not have been aware that a few new recruits had already joined and were undergoing induction. Similarly some others would not have known that Mr X had already resigned and left. In all HR reports therefore, earlier we used to check whether the sum total of employees is matching or not. One central agency was declared as the authority, and everybody else would adjust their data to it. This is because all of them were looking at different entities at data. Not in HRMS, when they look at the mirror image of a single pool of data. It will benefit immensly if you plan all your reports and MIS only from HRMS database.

4.16 Parallel Working to Save Time

When an employee separates, the separation module is run, and the information is flashed to all the several agencies that need to clear his final payment. Time, on account of sequential actions is saved and all decisions are taken in the shortest time possible.

4.17 Centralization and Decentralization Together

Suppose you have a fundamental parameter like nobody can be promoted in less than three years in the existing scale of pay, then the software would prevent such an order even if at client end somebody out of ignorance or otherwise does it. Similarly a central agency can always keep an eye on trend of promotions being given day after day.

4.18 Anybody Can Do the Work of a Specialist

For any HR manager, the data regarding family members of the employee is an important segment. Most of these members are dependent and many kind of employee services are extendable to them. Careful planning of a central table of dependents therefore shall contribute to decentralized use of the information for LTC, scholarships, medical treatment and final dues in case of unfortunate demise of the employee. In fact, the application will generate the specific list of dependents who are valid for the specific purpose.

4.19 No Need to Physically Send Any Report

When a new employee joins, vital and verified data about him are captured and fed into the HRMS system which auto-generates his unique employee number. With this, his details immediately flashes to all concerned sections at the same moment and all of them start doing their role simultaneously without waiting for the hard copy order.

Similarly in the Transfer module, the receiving department gets the employee data as soon as the person is released from the old department.

4.20 Decision Support System: Breaking the Limit of Hierarchical Decision Making

Where several parameters have to be checked many times by different experts, the role of an expert can be taken over by the computer to a good extent. For example while extending loan facilities, linkage with current pay, take home pay, admissible limits etc can be checked by the system before clearing the loan request.

Similarly in disciplinary action module, you would be notified of how many times disciplinary action has already been taken in the past, so that you can decide on his current charges.

4.21 Automatic Tracking: Events Announce Their Arrival by Themselves

In attaining the age of superannuation, the system clock enables instantaneous change and the status of employee changes from 'working' to superannuated. You do not have to check it every month from the register and do not need to inform several agencies who shouldn't deal with him as a working employee. No separate effort is required to check, inform or be informed. All relevant users come to know about, immediately if you have provided a system of alert.

4.22 Process Efficiency: Speed, Lesser Cycle Time

The qualities of instantaneous passage of digital information from one point to many points and also computerized checking of employee data enables dramatic improvement of cycle time of employee services.

4.23 Accuracy, Automatic Updating

Keeping the history of many events in the career of the employee is an important aspect of information. History of posts held from time to time, grades and pay allowed at different point of career are for example some of the relevant information which are often required of taking decisions at the later part of the career. The history building can emerge from the automatic archiving features of any HRMS database.

4.24 Convergence: Ensemble of Dissimilar Entities

Convergence is the trend in technologies to merge into new technologies that bring together a new creation. While historically, technology may handle one medium or accomplish one or two tasks, through technological convergence, devices are now able to present and interact with a wide array of media. For example, video was played on a television by using a video player of some sort, music was played on a tape deck or compact disc player, radio was played on an AM/FM tuner, and video games were played through a console of some sort. Voice conversation was carried on using a telephone. Now all these functionalities have been converged in a PC.

Analogous changes would be needed in HR. Periodic medical examination data and competency data can be used for deciding placement of employees individually as well as systems like placing in softer jobs. Similarly medical data can be blended with absenteeism, shift life, counselling activities.

4.25 Delegation

The Security Roles & Privileges, Passwords, Departments earmarked for specific HR Officers facilitate significant delegations. The potential of HRMS is not tapped fully if delegation is not done in the post computerization era.

4.26 Generic Office Systems

Availability of a single pool of HR data enables another employee a friendly step. Like in ATM, we can run a chain of global help centres, in less manpower, without presence of physical files, and any employee can walk up to any centre and enjoy the services.

Flow Chart 3

Designing HRMS Creatively

Areas to reduce paper copies

↓

Areas for consistency in reports

↓

Areas of parallel working to save time

↓

Implementing centralization and decentralization together

↓

Generalist doing the work of a specialist

↓

Eliminating physical dispatch of reports

↓

Delegation by decision support system

↓

Automatic tracking of HR events

↓

Accurate automatic updating

↓

Convergence of dissimilar entities

↓

Employee getting serviced in any office

The benefits of HRMS would be fully enjoyed if any subprocess in HR is filtered step by step in the flow chart - 3.

Once developed, the module on a computer screen displayed the following menu items:

Employee

Employee Information
Fresh recruitment

Personal information

Dependents
Addresses
Nominees for CPF/Gratuity
Emergency contact number
Qualifications
Past Employment details

Internal transfer
Career Profile
Grade history

Salary details

Separations
Deployment
Blood Group
Family Planning
Court cases
Spouse details
Reward details
Special pay details
Accident details
Detention details
Punishment history
Accident history
Vehicle details

Codifications

Areas
Zones
Departments
Sections
Executive designations
Non Executive designations
Sanction of posts
Lines of Promotion
Roster Points
Magic numbers
LTC LLTC Blocks

Institute
Loan codes
Dearness Allowances
Grades
Categories

Leave type

Help Screen
Non standard clusters
Heads of Departments
HR Officers
Circulars

MIS (Report & Graphics)

Superannuation notice
General Query
Superannuation list
Man power projections
Departments grade matrix
Executive graphics
Department Grade Graph
Retirement Graph
Sex Distribution Graph
Grade Graphs
Designation-wise Graph

Trainee

Trainee/Regularization

Estblishment Activities

Leave
Leave transaction

Special leave
Study leave
Maternity/Miscarriage

LTC

LTC LLTC Advance
LTC LLTC Sanction
LTC Statement
LTC Query

Promotion

Promotion Activities (Forms)
Screening Committee
Trade Test
DPC
Seniority
Merit Rating

Advances

Loan Advances & Miscellaneous
Festival Advances
Cycle Advances
Vehicle Advances
HRA Orders
LTE Sanction Orders

4.27 Codification of Employee Data

Codification aims at enabling standardized ways of storing and querying information. In HR field, there are two advantages. One is that instead of long string of texts if we use one-two digit numbers then the data entry operator can do his job much more easily. Similarly codes enable to users query very conveniently and accurately. Some examples are produced below:

a. Category Codes : One example of codifying the category of employees who are dealt as per different company and government rules and procedures are as under:

Category code	Description
1	General
2	Scheduled Caste (SC)
3	Scheduled Tribe(ST)
4	OBC (Other Backward Class)
7	LD (Locally Displaced)
15	Ex-serviceman
27	SC and Locally Displaced
25	SC and Ex-serviceman
363	ST, Physically Handicapped and LD

If we codify like given above, we can seek query for various attributes of employees who are ST, Handicapped and Locally Displaced by using the code 363.

b. Department Code : If we are establishing the HRMS in a very large employee base, then it is important to establish codes for the departments also. An employee will then belong to a department, department will be part of a bigger zone, zones in a division and division in to the whole organization. Conceptually, the code can be constructed like as under:

One digit for division	One digit for zone	Two digits for the department

When the Telecommunication department in a large plant is coded 1836, here 1 implies that it belongs to the division 1 (which say is Works), to a zone of 18 (which may mean electrical) and 36 as its unique code when read along with 1 and 8. Some more examples are as under:

Department code	Description of the code
1011	BLAST FURNACE in IRON zone of WORKS division
1201	Steel Melting Shop in STEEL zone of WORKS division
1421	Wire Rods MILL in MILLS zone of WORKS division
1613	Mechanical Heavy Maintenance in MECHANICAL zone of WORKS division
1802	POWER SYSTEMS in Power zone of WORKS division
2001	RCL in SERVICES zone of WORKS division
5006	BUSINESS PLANNING in ADMINISTRATION ZONE of non-works division
5222	Public Health Department in TOWN SERVICES ZONE of non-works division
5601	CONSTR. (TPL) CONSTRUCTION
5800	Rajhara mines in Iron Ore zone in MINES division

c. Qualification Code : Employees are recruited with a prescribed qualification base and new qualifications are added while in service. Qualification data of employees is an important HR data which is required for various manpower planning purposes. Therefore, it is important to establish codes for the employee qualifications also. Qualifications again have a hierarchy like PG, graduate, diploma, high school, illiteracy. Qualifications also have a horizontal spread which is called specialization in different fields. Methods of codification of qualification therefore should contain all these charactertics. Examples are as under:

QUALIFICATION _CODE	DESCRIPTION
0	ILLITERATE
1	NO SCHOOLING
11	CLASS I
12	CLASS II
13	CLASS III
14	CLASS IV
15	CLASS V
16	CLASS VI
17	CLASS VII
18	CLASS VIII
19	CLASS IX
30	CLASS X
31	MATRIC
107	SSC (matric)
41	HSC
40	HSSC
102	SSLC (class-11th)
101	PUC (class-12th)

42	I.A.
43	I.COM
44	I.Sc
45	B.COM (Ist)
46	B.A. (1st)
47	B.Sc (1st)
82	LVD LICENCE
81	HVD LICENCE
71	AITT
70	ITI
106	BTC (teacher trn)
114	B. P Ed.
56	B.ED
104	M ED
110	Cert. Lib. Sc.
109	B Lib Sc
115	M. LIB & INF. SCIENCE
33	BOILER ATTDT (SECOND CL)
34	BOILER ATTDT (FIRST CL)
118	BOILER OPERATION ENGINEER
78	MINING MATE
79	BLASTERS CERTIFICATE
80	MINES SURVEYORS' CERT (statutory)
77	M/FOREMAN CERT (statutory)
113	MINE MANAGER (2nd cl) (stat)
112	MINE MANAGER (1st cl) (stat)
119	Elect SC (HT) (Mines-Stat)
120	Elect SC (MV) (Mines-Stat)
48	SUB OFR. COURSE (statutory)

49	STN. OFR. COURSE (statutory)
32	D.O.COURSE
73	DIPLOMA
87	DSW
111	DBM
128	Exe Genl Mgt Prg
74	PG DIP
59	BBA
22	BJRNL (journalism-grad)
116	B.PHARMACY
117	B.MUSIC
50	B.A.
51	B.COM
57	B.HSc
52	B.Sc
200	BCA
60	M.A.
61	M.COM
66	M HSc
62	M.Sc
105	M Phil
64	Ph.D
68	MBA
58	LLB
203	LL.M
204	HSL ACCOUNTANT
76	ICWA
75	CA
199	CS (Company Sect)
72	DIP. in ENGG

67	MCA
108	AIC (Chem.engg)
201	AMIIChem.E
205	AMIME (Mech engg)
55	B.Sc (ENGG)
20	AMIE
21	AMIIM
54	B.E.
53	B.TECH
24	GRADUATESHIP (ENGG)
103	M.E
65	M.TECH
125	M.Sc. (ENGG)
37	D'CARDIO (Med-dip)
86	DOMS (Med-dip)
69	DCH (Med-dip)
95	DRM (Med-dip)
92	DCP (Med-dip)
91	DGO (Med-dip)
88	DLO (Med-dip)
38	DHA (Med-dip)
36	DVD (Med-dip)
97	DPM (Med-dip)
98	DIH (Med-dip)
35	DA (Med-dip)
100	D'ORTHO (Med-dip)
126	DTCD (Med-dip)
127	RAD_ELECT (Med-dip)
202	BAMS

85	MBBS (Med-grad)
123	B.V.Sc n A.H (Med-grad)
90	DNB (Med-pg)
39	MDS (Med-pg)
94	MD (Med-pg)
84	MS (Med-pg)
124	M.V.Sc n A.H (Med-pg)
96	MCH (Med-hpg)
93	DM (Med-hpg)
39	MDS (med-pg)
94	MD (med-pg)
84	MS (med-pg)

Separation and Other Status Codes

Employees separate from the organization naturally on reaching the age of superannuation. They also separate on tendering resignation, on natural/accidental death and many other reasons. Unlike the manual way of keeping employee records, the data of separated employees are not deleted from the records. In a computerized database, separated employees continue to exist but with 'separated' status as compared to the current employees having 'working' status. Different types of separation status need to be codified as it makes them eligible for different kinds of treatment. Similarly employees who are working, need to be categorized as to whether they are trainees or regulars, or whether they are under deputation. Similarly suspended and chargesheeted employees need to carry an appropriate status flag so that they are dealt differently in various HR processes. Examples of the codes are as under:

SEPARATION CODES	
CODE	DESCRIPTION

SA	TERMINATION/REMOVAL
SD	DISMISSAL
SE	EXPIRED
SG	RESIGNED
SM	PERMANENT MED. UNFIT
ST	TRANSFERED
SV	VOLUNTARY RETIREMENT
SR	SUPERANNUATION
SS	FORCED RETIREMENT

WORKING CODES	
CODES	DESCRIPTION
WW	WORKING
WC	C/SHEETED
WN	TRAINEE/NMR
WP	PUNISHMENT
WS	SUSPENDED
WL	SABBATICAL/STUDY LEAVE
WX	DEPUTATION WITH PAY
WY	DEPUTATION WITHOUT PAY

4.28 The Data Entry Process

When the forms were getting ready, we suddenly faced the problem of input data. The traditional information was existing in non-standard formats in geographically spread out locations. Things were available in the form of various documents like SB, PF, Registers. More recent ones were also existing as computer files in all varieties of formats and packages. Again in PC too they existed some where in word process files and elsewhere in spread sheets and dBase files.

The diversity of data sources were really frightening. We decided to transfer them in various stages to the new database.

Over a period of time, dBase file of all 55,000 employees could be prepared along with 16 vital data about each employee. These vital data were employee number, name, first name, second name (surname), grade, date of birth, date of joining, department, section, designation, category, date of entry into present grade, qualification, department, section, zone.

The seniority list which was regularly published for information of employees from time to time was a vital source. The computer files which were maintained by departments for multiple purposes in another sources. Finally the service book and personal files of the employees were also useful sources of information. The Service Book (10-12 pages) entered all vital entries made by PEs from time to time. The Personal Files sometimes ran up to 1000-1200 pages and each page contained somẹ event of his career. We decided that in order to begin the second phase data entry, we should start the data feeding with the first two sources. The bulky Personal File would be taken up afterwards. Combining the two systems (seniority list and PC files) a flat data file was prepared. The programmer then transferred all these data to the Oracle data base. The integrity constraints of the database were so strong that initially it accepted only 600 records out of 55,000. In a project like this we were advised that it may be useful to load data first and then check for anomalies.

A central HRMS section existed much earlier in the mid nineties. It soon became the main hub of these exciting activities. As the design work progressed to finalization, the section was becoming the lifeline of the department and was carrying out following important jobs:

- Training of executives and employees.
- General co-ordination with departments like Finance.
- Following up with RDCIS and C&IT in case of major software and hardware problems.

- Printing and distribution of voluminous reports.
- Updating of certain data for which field users do not have access to change.

Flow Chart 4

Data Sourcing and Data Entry

Formation of central HRMS section

↓

Finalizing norms of coalition with Finance and IT departments

↓

Identification of data sources

↓

Codification of data

↓

Data entry stage-1 as per hierarchy of importance of fields (for say 16 fields)

↓

Data entry stage-2 of other fields

↓

Data feeding and data loading from other databases

Chapter 5

KNOWING THE EMPLOYEE BETTER: THE TRANSITION PROCESS IN HRMS

5.16 Data Transfer System Involving HR and Finance after Comprehensive Verification

5.17 Infusing HRMS to Work Culture

5.1 Transition to HRMS as Change Management

For the magnitude of transformations that HRMS brings in any organization, the Human Resources practitioner has to follow all the professional steps of a change management situation. Firstly, he has to create a sense of urgency in the organization on the need of the proposed HRMS. In a large organization, change is possible if you are moving with a strong coalition of protagonists. It is therefore necessary one must organize into a close knit group which will do any thing for the changes to happen. Some of them would ally with you quickly because they grasp the vision. For most others you must propagate it. Communicating the vision of computer based employee services is an important task for the HRMS activist. Like in most major changes, there would be n number of obstacles and resistances. One must be alert about them and deal with them. For many stake holders a series quick benefits are alluring. From a status of passive onlookers, this will turn them into active supporters. One must therefore build on the initial achievements to accelerate change and finally embed new practices into the management culture. So we deal with the transition phase of HRMS into this format: creating a sense of urgency, forming of a strong coalition, communicating the vision, eliminating obstacles to change, demonstrating quick achievements, building on initial achievements to accelerate change, institutionalizing the new practices in the work culture.

5.2 History of Computer Applications in the Subject Organization

Before we get into details of these, it is time to understand the setting against which the change to HRMS was deployed. Some of these historical backgrounds are already spelt out in

Chapter-3. In this part of the book, a familiarization with the role of computers in local organization at different historical stages would be useful.

Phase 1 (1955-1970)

The first electronic computer system procured by the organization was an IBM 1401 machine procured in 1967. A new department of EDP (Electronic Data processing) was formed. Autocoder was the programming language and 16 K was the RAM memory of the machine. A FORTRAN evaluator was added later on for using FORTRAN programming language. The machine had peripherals like card reader, line printer and the tape devices. The activities which were taken up were Payroll or preparation of monthly salary bills of employees, calculations pertaining to Provident Fund (CPF), sales invoicing and inventory control in materials management

Phase 2 (1971-1990)

In 1979, a Russian machine EC1022 was hired on rental basis, which could use various languages like COBOL, PASCAL, PL1 and FORTRAN. However for most of the practical purposes, COBOL was used. With the installation of this machine all activities except payroll was shifted here. In 1988, the machine was returned back to the owner.

In January 1986, a new BURROUGHS machine was procured and installed. The machine had 9.3 MB RAM, 1 GB disc and was provided with two processors. With the installation of this machine all activities including payroll were transferred to it. The machine used COBOL as programming language and DMS2 as the database software. The activities undertaken through the above system were Store Accounts, Sales Accounts, estate related processes like house rent, electricity charges, CPF related processes, stores and purchase documentation, Voluntary Retirement scheme, Employees Family Benefit

Scheme, Central Accounts and Order Progress and sales invoice system in addition to already covered areas.

This period also witnessed emergence of Computerized Maintenance Management System [CMMS] as a separate IT department in 1981 . In an integrated steel plant, the diversity and the magnitude of the installed equipments call for a well defined, procedure-oriented and well documented system of maintenance which works smoothly. It is to satisfy these needs that the project Computerized Maintenance Management System (CMMS) was taken up for implementation. The system study and designing was done with the help of Czech consultants camping in a nearby town. The hardware procured was an ND server installed by ECIL with 36 terminals in different user departments. In the year 2000, the software was transferred to Oracle database, and Developer 2000 application was used. Currently the system is operated through more than 100 user PCs. The main advantages accrued with the implementation of CMMS were improvement in plant equipment availability, utilization and reduction equipment breakdowns.

INCOS (Integrated Control System), another department, was conceptualized in the year 1984 when automation and computerization was taken up by the Union Government as a thrust area. BSP was chosen as a model plant for full computerization. As per the plan, 300 crores rupees was sanctioned by SAIL for the project. The Department of Electronics GOI was the consulting agency for providing this module in association with Purdue, USA. As per the project, there were to be four hierarchical levels of automation viz Instrument level, PLC level (automation command), Supervisory control (over multiple PLCs of a department) and Area control/MIS. INCOS did not come up as per its original plan but has been handling many vital projects in different shops.

Phase 3 (1990-tll date)

The application of computers reached new heights with the advent of multipurpose PCs (Personal Computer) and better networking infrastructure. Two SUN server machines were procured in 1996 and all the applications were transferred to it in 1997. Subsequently two more SUN machines were added to it in the year 1999. Currently more than 1000 terminals are hooked to these machines spread over the industrial area and civil township. The area of application also spread horizontally to many green areas like human resources and financial accounting.

MMIS (Materials Management Information System) conceptualized in June 1991, aimed at comprehensive on-line integrated materials management and related financial processes. This includes bill passing, material accounts, cataloging more than 200,000 items, processing of average 8000 purchase indents in a month and stores accounts. Design was done in house. The process handled an average 56,000 consignments annually, 95,000 bills per annum and the value of transactions exceeded Rs. 500 crores. The original database used was VAX RDB, but in July 2001, the system was transferred to ORACLE 8i. This system involved about 300 user departments and 30,000 venders. There were 86 PC terminals connected to the MMIS server.

Traffic Management System abbreviated as "TRAMS" is an online system, which monitors the information needs of Rail Transport function of the Steel Plant. The internal transportation of materials and semi-finished goods in the plant is mainly handled by a fleet of 80 locomotives out of which an average of 60 is in operation at any point of time. TRAMS maintains online information pertaining to all railway wagons, steel plant wagons, locomotives and permanent way. The modus operandi of the system is to get hold of the data relating to traffic parameters right at the source of activity, so as to eliminate the human communication error.

A similar application of OASIS (ORDER PROGRESSING & SALES INVOICING SYSTEM) covers the functions of as many as ten departments of marketing department, Research & control lab, Traffic department, Sales accounts, BBM, MM, RSM, WRM and PM. The project was initiated with main objectives of better centralized control of loading and dispatches, on-line help for shipping section for destination-wise loading and rake formation decision, to avoid codification and re-entry of invoice data enabling EDP to print invoices without going through punching of data, memos to be communicated to shipping sections immediately after the testing. This also eliminates the manpower required for the transfer of memos between the testing laboratories and mills shipping and on-line generation of railway receipts.

The Finance function also took up a number of projects for computerization during the second half of the nineties which include voucher management, operation accounts and raw material accounting.

It is against the above setting that HRMS emerged in the late nineties.

5.3 Creating a Climate for Change and a Sense of Urgency for HRMS

HRMS is to be viewed as a pervasive change in the organization and accordingly managerial steps have to be taken. In a project like HRMS, large number of members of the HR team must act with sufficient urgency. The feel of urgency in the instant case was achieved by projecting the following scenarios:

a. The depleting manpower in the HR department which originally had 400 executives and staff was fast decreasing due to superannuation whereas employee development load on the department was rapidly increasing.

b. New recruitments of staff were not desirable because of rising manpower cost.
c. The existing staff and executives spent a good part of daily life in routine, repetitive jobs whereas the development and strategic areas were suffering.
d. The pay days and a few days there after drew lot of employees flooding HR offices and query about error in salary administration. Unlike other computerization projects, this is one project where computer will directly help the grass root employees.

These messages had logic with emotion and enabled HR department collective to see the enormity of solution possible through HRMS.

5.4 Core Implementation Team of HR, Finance and IT

In gigantic organizations, change is smoother if you are moving with a strong coalition of protagonists. One can not do it alone. Successfully achieving the change objectives takes more than one individual or even one team. It is therefore necessary that one must organize into a close knit group which will do any thing for the change to happen. Some of the members would ally very quickly because they grasp the vision and this is what happened in our case.

In this case, the team consisted two to three executives each from HR, C&IT and R&D. The commonality in the team was that we all valued a concern as to how can the HR manager aspire to be a change agent of work culture when the most modern tool of science is not adequately available to him? There were a few transfers in the core group or time perused and also occasional times of conflict within. But at the end of the day we all enjoyed a reflective environment working on the excitement of the newness of the project.

In major change events, many people would feel immediately uncomfortable. The main engine that will drive a neat transition to the HRMS environment is a very close and healthy relationship between HR department, the system developing department like C&IT and departments like Finance which are partner service providers. In our case, situation was little bit more complex as the system developing agency itself were two different organizations. One was the RDCIS, the R&D wing who designed the basic modules of HRMS, and the other, the local C&IT department who built on the base modules and also designed extensive customization.

We had our first taste of re-engineering with implementation of 'Integrated HR Payroll Technology'. There are many administrative activities where both HR and Finance departments are involved. For example, when an employee is promoted, the promotion decision is taken in the HR department, His increase in salary is also decided in the HR department. HR prepares a report for departmental promotion committee on which decisions on promotion is taken. Thereafter, HR issues an administrative order on promotion to the employee, which is sent to Finance carrying the promotion decision and fixation of the revised salary of the employee. The Finance used to recheck the calculations, feed the data into their Payroll system and just before salary day used to send the advice to the employee's bank accordingly. The analogical transactions take place in many other areas like grant of various allowances (like HRA), reimbursement of expenditures (like LTE), incentives etc.

With the introduction of the HRMS, which covers automation of bulk of the HR administration, it was felt by many that Finance as a sequential intermediary in salary administration, may not be necessary as the decision making and salary calculation in HR is done error free by the computer. Also re-feeding the data at Finance end into Payroll system had the potential for error in feeding. This argument appeared as a wild imagination in the first look. But as implementation proceeded module after module, this started assuming an earthly form.

Appreciating that there is no practical value addition in the above process at Finance end, the Payroll was directly connected to HRMS. As per the revised system, when HR officer decided a promotion on his computer terminal, the revised salary directly updated the Payroll. Apart from efficiency in terms of time and accuracy, the system also rendered free the entire group of Finance personnel, who were engaged full time in verification and data feeding. It created a win-win situation for both HR & Finance.

5.5 HR Payroll Process : Data Transfer And Sharing

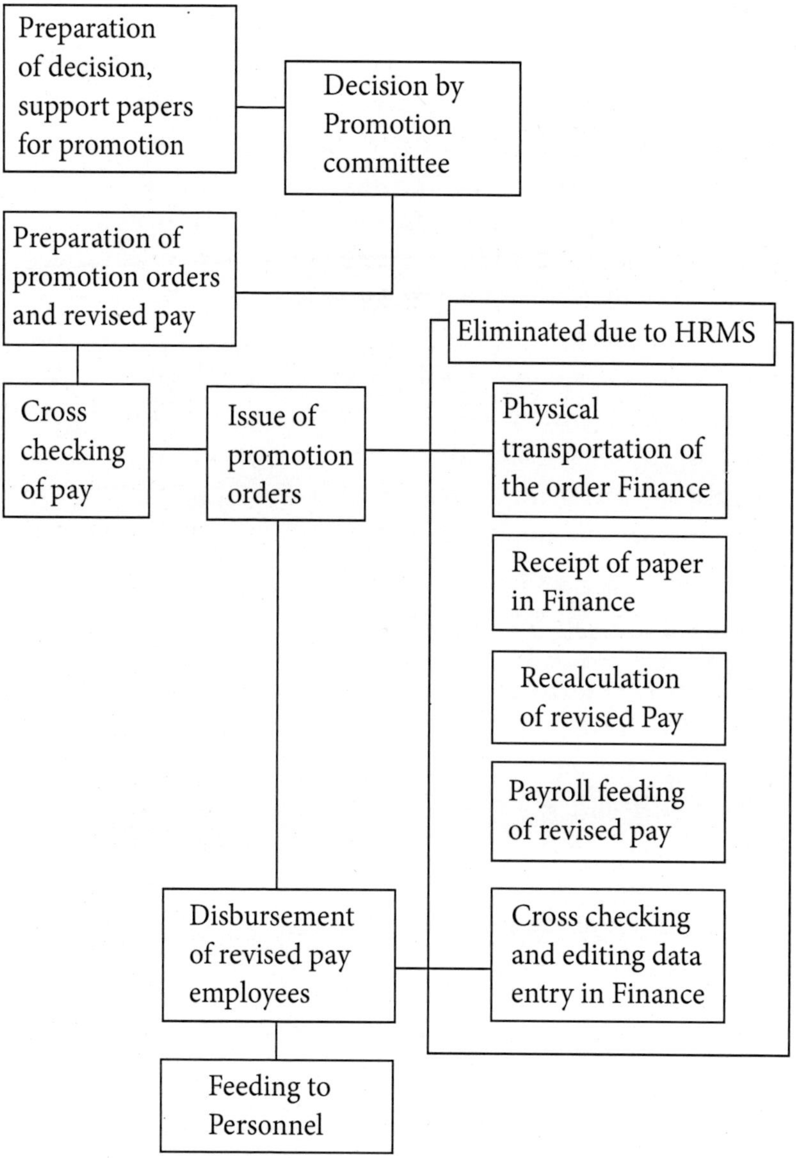

Let us have a look at the following major learning from the case which succeeded as generation and implementation of a novel idea.

It is not necessary that a good suggestion can be evolved and implemented by a homogenous group belonging to the same section or the department only. In this case the idea took shape with contribution from people from disparate departments having engineering, computer, finance and personnel background. The idea was also not formed in a single session, it acquired meaning over a period of time as various advantages of the proposal was appreciated.

The idea was nurtured and put to shape even when the issue was so important which can only be decided by top management. The implications were very radical. Salary and wage disbursement is one of the age old functions of Finance department. Therefore the issue of making financial disbursement to employees without routing through Finance is something unimaginable then. Similarly, making the HR department 100% accountable on salary distribution was quite unprecedented. In normal scenario, such a decision will be a major one. The group continued to work on the concept with great deal of risk.

There was no structured approach to design the proposal. The framework evolved in disjointed manner. Like jigsaw puzzle, pieces were added one by one, meeting after meeting.

The group pursued the implementation even when there was a great deal of risk involved. The point here was to provide full financial powers to the HR officers relating to the salary of the employees without any mediation by Finance function. The failure of the plan could have led to disastrous ends.

Obsession with one's own function, lack of awareness of the perspectives of other departments and professional jealousy normally hamper a smooth switch over to a new work system.

But the joy of experimenting something new and being partners on a novel project would help in team-building. A good team work will help you to overcome minor and major problems in the software in the transition phase.

Therefore regular and prolonged meetings between all the cross-functional teams should take place. Contents in a typical meeting on data transfer from HRMS to Payroll should be as given in the box:

Typical points discussed on sharing of computerized data among HR, IT and Finance
1. All administrative orders would be issued through HRMS and never on standalone/manual system. 2. A summary screen on the changes due to above will be given to Wages and HR Department to scroll through. 3. A fixed day in the month (say 22nd) to be agreed when the data would be transferred. 4. Wages can cross check the data with the hardcopies received subsequently in Central Wages from various personnel offices. 5. Provision to delete records/add records and modify records in the screen would be given to the Personnel department. This would be done by modifying the original records in HRMS database by the Personnel Department. 6. Printouts after action would be kept in the wages section for records with a copy to the Personnel Department on a fixed day every month. 7. From screen at 5 after modifications if any by the Personnel department, the data in existing formats will be sent to payroll files (data file) to update. 8. Payroll master may be updated from data available at above and the update report is sent to Wages for records.

Flow Chart 5

Periodic Data transfer and sharing

Making it mandatory to issue all administrative orders through HRMS.

↓

Data would be transferred on a fixed day of the month from HR to Finance.

↓

Mirror screen on the changes happening given to Finance Department to view

↓

Finance cross-checking the data with the hardcopies received subsequently

↓

Feedback to Personnel Department

↓

After modifications if any by Personnel department, the data is sent to payroll files to update.

↓

Payroll master is updated from above data and update report is sent to Wages for records

5.6 Collaboration within HR: Chasing a Shared Dream

A shared urgency for change may compel most people for action, but it is the vision that steers a collective in the right direction. The direction of change is equally important as the momentum. A good vision or dream provides a inspiring, motivating picture of future. It clarifies the general direction of change and aligns the behaviour of the people. This vision apart from clarity should contain elements of futurism, be compelling, realistic, focussed and flexible.

We accordingly designed and communicated a dream to various stakeholders which we used to refer as the CPO (Computerised Personnel Office) dream .

When you are a member of very large HR team distributed widely in different subfunctions and several field offices, you need to have a strong coalition within your department.

One way to make allies within department is to demonstrate loudly the first set of advantages. In the case of integrated HR-Payroll system of HRMS, we announced the following benefits:

a. Quicker disbursement of benefits to employees
b. Work is simplified in as much as all intermediary and manual steps in Finance and C&IT are taken out.
c. Direct control over the salary of the promoted employees by the personnel executives.

The initial days of experimenting were both horrible as well as humorous.

The truth logic codes of '1' and '0' as true and false were not clear to many HR executives and as a result there were real chaotic situations in salary distribution in the beginning. In a database of 55,000 employees every month during salary days, there will be angry complaints of several wrong payments. There was an extreme case where an executive applied for HRA (House Rent Allowance), was paid the same, but by mistake his LTE was withdrawn. Next month as a corrective action when LTE was restored, HRA got withdrawn.

Reason for such error can be any of the followings:

a. Mistake in feeding in HRMS system.
b. Mistake in running HRMS application.
c. Non-receipt of hard copy orders in the computer points.

Designing a lovable vision and communicating it across helps a large group of people to orchestrate their thought and action for a fast implementation of change. So we communicated an idea to our group which in those days we used to call as the CPO dream.

5.7 The Computerized HR Office Dream

The CPO Dream

HUMAN RESOURCES INFORMATION SYSTEM

COMPUTERIZED PERSONNEL OFFICES [CPO]

-a concept paper-

Function:

To carry out establishment related and employee services jobs of personnel office through the computerized application of HRMS.

Locations:

The CPOs will be operated at nine locations of plant. They will be geographically spreadout so as to generally maintain a minimal distance from major departments. In addition, there will be three locations in the outside works area.

Realignment of offices:

Existing office resources will be realigned in following two alternatives in order of preference:

1. Two or three existing offices may be merged comprehensively along with staff and all records.

2. Regular offices can continue in their existing locations. One authorized staff of each office will be camped in the terminal location for handling HRMS related activities. In this alternative, the additional job of sending papers to terminal point is to be handled.

Executive manning:

Each office initially will be manned by two personnel executives. One of them, [preferably the junior one] will handle establishment matters through HRMS application with an authorized user code. The senior one will deal with HRD and IR related issues. There need not be a reporting relationship between the two and they can report directly to the zonal head. There will thus be 18 personnel executives for works excluding the zonal heads.

Office staff:

Each CPO will have two staff authorized to work in HRMS application. The personnel services of works area will therefore be managed by say 18 office staff. With large scale checks and balance available in the HRMS package, most of the computer operation jobs would be left to the staff roles. Personnel executive may be required to operate computer only for higher orders jobs like promotion etc. In the first hours of the day, the personnel executive will get a feedback report on jobs handled in the previous day. Keeping in view the fact that the role of the identified group of staff will be pivotal to the success of the system, their selection, training and motivation is of paramount significance. Utilization and attitudinal aspects of other staff are to be judiciously planned out.

Simplification of procedures:

Procedures are to be simplified so that there is minimal involvement of other-than-personnel-agencies. Repeated reference to HOD on issues where practically no decision-making is involved are to be cut down.

Minimal paper work:

Only one copy of all administrative orders will be issued by computerized personnel offices to be given to the employee.

All communication to Finance will be given electronically in a composite list of additions, separations, variations (including promotions, regularizations) and advances including LTC etc. This list will be offloaded to Finance twice in a day at standard hours.

The service book will be referenced only in very selected occasions like court cases etc.

Interfacing with other agencies:

The HODs and union officials are to be exposed to the various aspects of the project so that an appropriate atmosphere is available for introducing the change.

Security:

An elaborate system of time stamping of selected activities will be introduced to ensure accountability of all computer based activity.

Data discipline:

After the input forms are entered into the system, employee wise data sheets containing comprehensive information available in HRMS will be generated and the copy along with the endorsement of concerned dealing asst will be kept in the personnel file.

Ultimate flexibility in Personnel Services:

Initially, each CPO will cater to employees of a specific group (departments). After the system stabilizes, we can introduce a facility of personnel service to employees in any CPO.

5.8 Enabling Actions for HRMS

New structures, new skills and new systems need to be in place so that the change intervention is supported adequately. The HRMS strategist has to think about their organization's capabilities as carefully as they think about individual people's capabilities.

Regarding training of executives and non-executives, data entry and report generation skills are not difficult to learn. But in those days it was really difficult to locate a staff in each office who can properly handle a keyboard. We took help from the local chapter of Computer Society of India and held one week programs for the select staffs and executives. As time passed, many others also got interested and in two years time we could cover all.

Executives soon realized that the future has no escape from computer. Most of these came forward and participated in the week long training.

Keeping in view that usage of computer needs a proper logical attitude, operational discipline, a master plan for training all those involved in the implementation was drawn out. In a period of one year, 110 persons of HR department drawn from senior, middle, frontline management as well as office staff were imparted training in data base management.

5.9 The Role of Central HRMS Section

The role of central HRMS is to plan, organize, coordinate and control the user processes in the HR department. As the implementation progresses job becomes more and more complex; but at the end of the day its very inspiring. Designing building blocks for future of HR can be a very rewarding experience.

The section initially therefore is headed by a person of HR Manager rank might grow in size and complexity to have a Dy General Manager as incharge.

The role of this group is as under:

a. Awareness programs for all executives and non-executives.
b. Action on mismatch of data between HR and Payroll.
c. Proper connectivity of terminals of personnel executives.
d. Liasioning with C&IT for necessary changes in the forms as per user feedback.
e. SOPs are issued and communicated in time.
f. Preparation of monthly plans about updating.
g. Supervising periodic transfer of data to Finance.
h. Inventory of PCs.
i. Inventory of computer stationeries and consumables.
j. Reports generation and MIS : different frequencies.
k. Instant answer to data queries.

l. Maintenance of HRMS website.
m. Various value added product.

The functioning of the central HRMS Section is complimented by the C&IT experts which carries out the following functions :

a. Creation of database.
b. Manage and upscale the database.
c. Manage storage allocation.
d. Manage roles.
e. Backups.
f. Oversee data entry.

5.10 Stakeholders Communication

Communicating the vision of computer based employee services is an important task for the HRMS activist. This communication is to address to all stakeholders like top management, HR officers, HODs, functional heads especially the Finance, unions and employees. They all need to be communicated in a variety of content, depth and details as given in the next page.

Table

Stakeholder/ Level of communication	aware	under-stand	colla-borate	commit
Top management		under-stand		
HR officers				commit

HODs	aware			
Finance			colla-borate	
Unions	aware			
Employees		under-stand		

We made a definite plan to involve the top management at 'understanding' level, i.e. higher than awareness level. This was required as we were seeking investment decisions from top management for the project. Also this sensitized them to approve several procedure changes which were needed as part of the HRMS based re-engineering plan.

For the employees, fortunately we already had a forum called 'Shop Communication Forum'. We utilized this forum as our platform to demonstrate the user end benefits to the employees.

The role of 'Finance' was much more active than other stake holders, the role of a collaborator. At a particular peak time, we used to even have daily meeting with them for detailed sharing of the project status.

The entire strategy of HRMS was based on the 'commitment' to it by the HR team. Therefore communication to them was both in depth as well as in divergent modes; written circular, review meeting, training as well as evaluation of their skill base.

For the HOD, to accept HRMS as a system needed less effort. Living in a technology world, most of them were already aware of potentials of computerization and they could quickly relate the need for the same in administration. In addition a pamphlet highlighting the efficiency of the new system was printed and circulated among the managers.

For the union, We had a couple of demo sessions involving all the top hierarchy. We felt this should be done as the implementation will ultimately lead to many procedural changes. Their acceptance of the system will always be of great help. In return, they sided with us when in the beginning there were many erroneous payments to some employees due to wrong handling of the database forms.

5.11 Short Term benefits

In successful change efforts, the protagonists create short-term victories; small but visible successes that nourish faith in change effort, mentally reward the hard workers, keep the critics at a distance, and build momentum. For HRMS, in concrete terms, it will have following advantages:

- Evidence that the HRMS plan is working.
- Approach is tested against real work organization.
- Help keep leaders and stake holders on board.
- Gradually silence the critics.

The HRMS strategist may find this step as one of the most difficult one and has to decide on a mix of simple and small pay off actions as well as some visible ones with big pay offs. Several steps were taken in this direction as may be seen from following examples:

a. Generation of any employee report from any of the more than forty offices on 24×7 basis.
b. Data sheets given to employees for self-check first time enabled employees for the first time to have a comprehensive look at their own information.
c. Crediting of increased pay to employees' bank account immediately after promotion.
d. Crediting of final payment to bank account after superannuation.

5.12 Implementing and Sustaining the Change: Handling the Resistance

There were innumerable numbers of obstacles and resistances as it happens with any new projects. They were mostly in the form of data error and mal-operation by users, wrong payments to employees, and wrong transactions to payroll. The core implementation team tried to handle each of them professionally, remained focussed, sustained the momentum and kept a close tab on the process while ensuring that such cases are not repeated.

5.13 Trials and Deadlines

Initially for some time all users in HR are allowed to play with the data and new computerized objects. But after that it has to follow live trials and deadlines for switch over to mandatory computerized processes. We had tragically observed elsewhere various powerful packages lying unused and neglected as the system did not make them use compulsorily. We did not want this to happen with us, and after a few months of parallel working, wanted to discard the old manual options.

Trials initially started with fictitious data in the central HRMS. We had many field HR officers who voluntarily participated in measuring the correctness of processing in the system and based on their feedback the software experts would be finetuning the packages.

The live data trials also started in central HRMS section and after a couple of months was launched in two field locations. The system was continuously fine-tuned with feedback from groups after groups. The hot trial with live data in other zones' terminal came up soon after.

Flow Chart - 6

Trials and deadlines

Trials with fictitious data in the central HRMS.

↓

Allow users to play with the data and new computerized objects.

↓

The live data trials in central HRMS section – module by module

↓

The live data trials in two/three field locations

↓

feedback from groups after groups, and quick customization

↓

Parallel running of computerized and manual systems

↓

Deadlines are declared for mandatory use after the trials

After we were satisfied with live trials for a couple of months, the deadlines were declared. It may be useful to have a look at the template of the administrative orders on the deadline:

Deadlines to make HRMS usage mandatory

Employee Data in HRMS Database

Based on interaction with all the groups of personnel executives of works and non-works, it has been decided that the employee data in HRMS database will be frozen on ________.

HR executives and dealing assistants are required to complete the data verification, comparison with personal file and updating jobs by this date. They are also needed to update the relevant fields regularly on day to day basis.

All HR executives may please note that following implications of the decision:

- The computerized data will now be directly utilized in various live transactions including in payroll
- Any discrepancy in data will evidently lead to anomalies of various kind and the accountability will lie largely with shop HR offices.
- After the deadline, the system will not accept any direct correction of data at shop terminals.
- Any exceptional cases where data is to be directly changed after the date may be sent to HRMS after obtaining the approval of the higher authority.

Central HRMS Section will liase with C&IT and Finance and ensure systematic processing of data.

5.14 Eliminating Obstacles to Change: Data Verification

Data Verification process is the most painful stage of HRMS implementation and based on our experience, we feel it should be the strongest obstacle to be tackled in the read to implementation of HRMS.

It is said that normally two or five percent error creeps in any case of large volume data events. Unverified data will cause very serious blunders and such blunders can cripple implementation of HRMS specially in areas which have Financial and IR implications. It would be strategic to microplan the verification process in three stages as shown below:

Sequence of Data Feeding and Data Verification

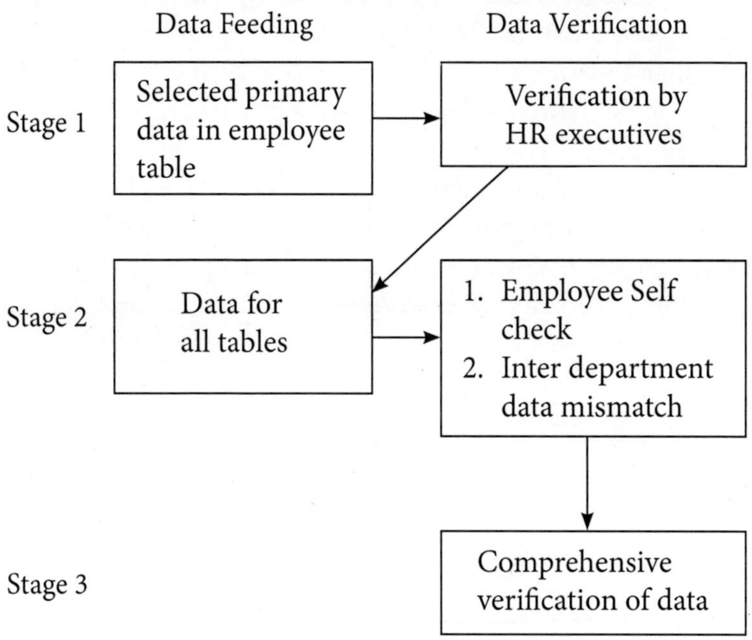

Fact remains that if you have a list of 150 fields of data for 50,000 employees, you will get dizzy as to how to approach for verification. Here we applied and recommended the norm of hierarchy of importance of data and stages of verification, as given in the preceding diagram.

Accordingly we undertook the verification process in three phases.

First time after the 16 primary information of employees were fed into the computer system, the prints were given to all site offices for verification from their personal records. After necessary correction on the sheets, the changes were centrally fed in the database.

During this period as the packages were still being developed, the central HRMS could generate some special purpose MIS, which exposed areas of weakness in data. The user HR officers would also get into a circle of use, verify, correct, re-use. For example, it can be useful to draw a list of employees who are say less than 16 years of age (minimum entry level) or more than 58 years of age (retirement age) and in the process reach the targets of error in data of birth entry.

After the 16 core information were verified, and site offices started to enter the balance data based on the Service Book and Personal File. This was a difficult time as they really created an additional load on each executive who had to carry out the task in addition to his normal day to day task. After a whole lot of monitoring this could be completed in a year's time.

Flow Chart 9A

Data Verification (Stage-1)

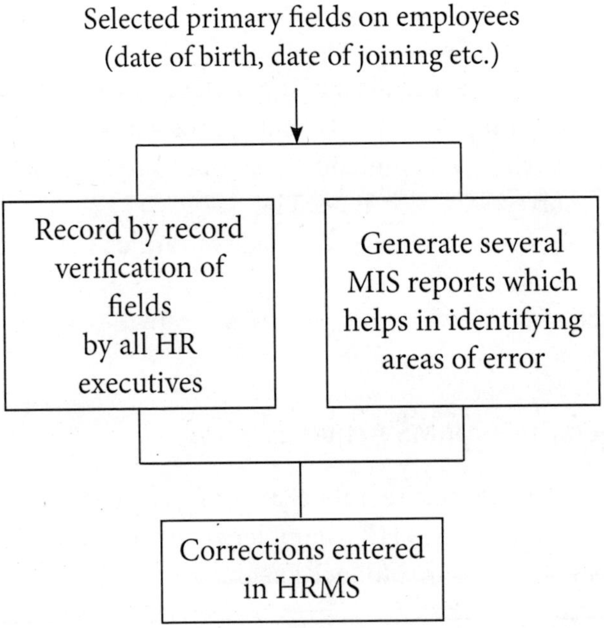

The volume of data was enormous. Therefore, it was necessary to verify the correctness of data. The job of data verification was mamoth. At this stage a novel idea was thrown up by an HR executive that except for sensitive information like date of birth, date of joining, qualification etc. balance data can be self-checked by the employees themselves. This was agreed to and the two large page employee data printouts were circulated requesting them to verify and return with corrections if needed. This way the second phase verification could be completed in six months' time.

Soon after, in order to strengthen the verification process five internal audit teams were formed who had following terms of references:

- Consistency of employee data in the computer system with the data in personal file/service book/paper documents.
- Correctness of all vital data pertaining to the employees including date of birth and date of joining.
- Specific recommendations for organization wide corrective action if need be.
- Assessment of progress made in various HRMS related activities.

Due to sudden bunching of HRMS activities a role clarity circular was issued as under:

Role-Clarity in HRMS Activities

With a view to ensure role-clarity in carrying out various activities pertaining to HR Computerization, the role clarity for different positions are produced below:

Sl no	Position	Role description in the context of Computerization
1	HR executives in Regular Personnel Offices (RPO) i.e. where HRMS terminals do not exist.	• Distribution and collection of employee checklist data sheets • Verification of all data in the employees checklist, seniority list and SPV reports against basic records. • Forwarding of copy of administrative orders/ documents effecting day to day changes in employee's status to concerned HRMS terminal.

2	HR executives in Computerized Personnel Office (CPO) i.e where HRMS terminals exist	• Generating various reports for all depts covered by the terminal for checking and final use. • Updating of the computer database on the basis of administrative orders/ documents received from all departments in configuration. • Care and safe upkeep of hardware. • Raising complains to C&IT in case of system failures.
3	HRMS section	• General co-ordination pertaining to HRMS activities • Following up with C&IT in case of major software and hardware problems • Printing and distribution of voluminous reports • Updating of certain data for which site users do not have access to change.
4	Zonal personnel heads	• Periodic review of performance of terminals. • Interventions where regular updating does not take place. • Audit of data in HRMS

Data verification became very complex as HRMS grew in size and number of transactions. We realized that the data we are checking isn't static but is changing with every passing hour and these on-going changes in data are also to be incorporated in the database as we are verifying the correctness of data. Below is a checklist procedure issued to keep a balanced tab on both verification and updating:

Checklist on Updating of Data

a. Employee Checklist Data

Sl no	Activity	Responsi-bility	YES/ NO
1	Employee data printouts have been supplied to all HR executives.	CHRMS	
2	Checklists have been distributed to all employees.	RPO	If not, reason and number
3	Checklists have been received back from all employees.	RPO	-do-
4	Corrections indicated by employees in the checklist has been verified against basic records of personnel office by dealing staff.	RPO	-do-
5	HR executive to check a good sample (Min. 30%) of documents. Sample size may be increased if the frequency of errors is high.	RPO	
6	Corrections entered in the HRMS database.	CPO	

b. Seniority List Data

Sl no	Activity	Responsi-bility	YES/ NO
7	Seniority list with career history data has been obtained from CHRMS.	RPO	
8	Prints have been checked and duly endorsed by dealing assts and HR officer.	RPO	
9	Corrections have been made in the computer database and HRMS section has been informed to generate final lists.	CPO	
10	Final prints of seniority list have been generated.	HRMS	
11	Final prints of seniority list have been published, checked and displayed for employees.	RPO	

c. Statistical Reports Data

Sl no	Activity	Responsi-bility	YES/ NO
12	The department level manpower position in database is tallying with basic records including breakups for casual trainees, regular employees.	RPO	If not, details
13	Reports have been checked and duly endorsed by the concerned dealing staff and personnel officer.	RPO	
14	Corrections if any, have been incorporated in the database.	CPO	
15	Final printouts are being generated periodically for use in p.o. office.	CPO	

d. Day to Day Changes

Sl no	Activity	Responsi-bility	YES/ NO
16	The changes that have taken place in the data during the period between filling of biodata forms and computer feeding, have been compiled.	RPO	
17	The above changes have been incorporated in the computer database.	CPO	If yes, up to what period
18	Copies of administrative orders/ documents affecting changes in employee's status are being sent to the concerned HRMS terminal on day to day basis	RPO	
19	Copies of above orders are being received	CPO	
20	Updations based on above orders are being entered into computer on daily basis.	CPO	

C.P.O = Computerised Personnel Office i.e. where HRMS terminal exist.

R.P.O = Regular Personnel Office i.e. where HRMS terminal does not exist.

Flow Chart 9B

Verification of Data (Stage 2)

Employee Self-check

Employee data printouts generated

↓

Printouts are supplied to all HR executives by HRMS

↓

Checklists are distributed to all employees by RPO

↓

Checklists are received back from employees by RPO

↓

Corrections indicated by employees in the checklist are verified against basic records of personnel office by dealing staff in RPO

↓

Personnel executive to check a good sample (Min. 30%) of documents. Sample size may be increased if the frequency of errors is found high in RPO

↓

Correction entered in the database in CPO

Flow Chart 9C

Verification through MIS

Manpower reports for all sections have been printed in CPO

↓

Reports have been checked and duly endorsed by the concerned dealing staff and personnel officer in RPO

↓

Check that department level manpower position in database is tallying with basic records including the standard breakups in RPO

↓

Corrections if any have been incorporated in the database by CPO

↓

Check that final printouts are generated periodically for use in HR office

Flow Chart 9D

(Day to Day Changes in Employee Data)

Copies of administrative orders on all changes are being received regularly in CPO

↓

Updations based on above orders are being made in the database on daily basis in CPO

One of the most significant changes in HRMS database happens because of joining of new members in the organization on account of new recruits, re-appointment employees and employees joining on transfer from other units. Their verification of data can take place in Recruitment Section itself as show below:

Flow Chart 10

Capturing Data of New Entrants

Filling Up Of Bio-Data forms in Recruitment cell

↓

Verification of data in Recruitment Section

↓

Submission of Joining Report in Recruitment Cell

↓

Autogeneration of personnel number after entering not-null fields

↓

Entering the Data in HRMS

↓

Data entry of comprehensive information of the employees in the training institute

5.15 Procedure for comprehensive verification

After HRMS came into existence for some period, a final round of verification of data should be carried out expanding the domain to all vital information of the employees.

This might appear as an extra work, but the organization looking to offload the administrative activities to HRMS automation are advised to carry out a phase-3 of data verification. In retrospect this appears today as the most painful part of the HRMS process. But there is perhaps no other option as unless the verification is done, we could not possibly switch over to independence from the paper files.

In our case, the fields for verification were as under:

Name
Father's Name
Sex
Marital Status
Grade, Grade Date, Basic Pay, Increment Date
Pay History
Regular Cadre Date
Hometown
Change in Home Town
Recruitment Type
Governing Rule
Leave Rule
Blood Group
Religion
Vehicle No., Sanction Date
Vehicle Details
HRA
Date of Birth
Date of Joining
Category (Caste)
Educational Qualification
Professional Qualification
Other Pays
Grades Held in Past
Dependents
Nominees (Gratuity/CPF)
Penalty
Present Address

Permanent Address
Discountable Service
Sabbatical Period
Family Planning
Probation
Medical Status
Duplicate Gate Pass
Surety
National Awards

The guideline issued listed the specific documents to be verified against each of the items.

The guidelines to HR offices covered the following aspects:

1. Checking records of all employees and covering discrepancies.
2. Matching and correcting all employee data as available in HRMS with data from personal records and feed corrections in HRMS through a specially defined HRMS module.
3. Prune personal files by removing disposable documents.
4. Carry out all HR functions on-line and reduce paper work.
5. Move towards a total paperless working.

5.16 Data transfer system involving HR and Finance after comprehensive verification

The template of data transfer processes after all the three stages of verification may be as under:

Revised Procedure for Data Transfer between HRMS [Personnel] and Payroll [Finance]

1.0 Objectives:

1.1 To avail the speed and accuracy advantages of the computer systems in EDP, Finance and Personnel in the field of various employee services through integrated solutions.

1.2 To minimize paper transmission of financial and personnel data, and achieve data capture at the source.

2.0 Data Transfer from HRMS To Payroll/Finance:

2.1 Employee Addition data

2.1.1 Primary data regarding any new person joining (new recruits and transferees from sister units) will be entered into HRMS database by the HR executive of the department where the new entrant submits his joining report. The data feeding will be done in the concerned HRMS terminal and autogenerated personnel number will be allotted by Central HRMS Section in Personnel.

2.1.2 Hard copy of the joining order will be issued by the above personnel executive addressed to Personal File, the Individual, Finance (concerned wages) and Time Office.

2.1.3 The data on the new inductee comprising of Plno, Name, Date of Joining, Date of Birth, Grade, Basic, DNI, Incentive Code, Bill No will be transferred electronically to Payroll on a fixed day of every month for preparation of salary.

2.1.4 Central HRMS section in Personnel will receive a monthly edit list from Payroll on these new records.

2.2 Employee Separation Data

2.2.1 Personnel executives will issue computerized administrative orders on employee separations

(Superannuation, VR, Death, Medical Unfitness, Resignation, Removal, Dissmissal etc.) concurrently with updating of the HRMS database. In case of retirement, a superannuation notice will be issued by the concerned personnel executive six months in advance. Superannuation order will be issued two months in advance.

2.2.2 Four hard copies of such orders will be generated from the concerned personnel office and these copies will be sent to Individual/nominee, Personal File, Finance and Time Office.

2.2.3 On weekly basis (every Monday), FSS in Personnel dept will centrally generate a consolidated list of the separated employees during the preceding week and one copy of the listing will be sent to all clearing agencies. Only in case of superannuation, the list will be generated one month in advance. These agencies will forward the No Dues Certificates to Final Claim Cell based on the above mentioned list and Final Settlement Section will issue suitable clearances to FCC for final payments accordingly.

2.2.4 When VR scheme is in operation, the VR data for the month will be electronically transmitted to Payroll each month containing the data for the preceding period. The supplementary VR data for the period 23rd to last day of the month will be given to Payroll along with separation data of the subsequent month.

2.2.5 Central HRMS section will receive a monthly edit list on these data from payroll.

2.3 Data on Employee Status Change:

2.3.1 HR executives will issue the administrative orders through the HRMS module which alters the status of employees including in the case of promotion, redesignation, punishment, regularization of trainees, internal transfers etc.

2.3.2 In case of promotion and redesignation, respective personnel executives will generate the DPC/Screening Committee report before the prescribed date of promotion. After the DPC/Screening report is cleared by the committee, the HRMS module will be run by the concerned HR executives to update the tables and the administrative orders will be generated. Hard copies of promotion/redesignation order will be sent to the employee, personal file, concerned wages and time office. The plno, new designation, new grade, new basic, new increment date of all the employees promoted/ will be electronically transferred to payroll on pre-notified dates.

2.3.3 Similarly, all concerned HRMS tables will be updated by the users in Personnel department concurrently with issue of administrative orders on punishment, regularization and internal transfers. The data on all such employees will be electronically transferred to payroll on a fixed date every month.

2.3.4 The Finance (wages) sections will not feed any data regarding employee status change. However, discrepancy if any noticed, can be referred by wages section to the concerned personnel executive who will take suitable further action on review.

2.3.5 Central HRMS section will receive a monthly edit list from Payroll containing all details which has been updated.

3.0 Data Transfer From Payroll To HRMS:

3.1 Data on Basic, DNI and Loan and Advance indicators will be updated from Payroll to HRMS on every 25th January and 25th July for records where Payroll's salary value is higher than that of HRMS except for employees under punishment or suspension. This is required as Payroll automatically updates the data based on dates of increment or monthly deduction of premium.

3.2 Local address data in the 'Addresses' table of HRMS will also be updated on above dates only for employees who are holding company accommodation.

4.0 General:

4.1 This revised procedure will be put to trial run from ________ and would be fully effective from ________.

4.2 Monthly review on the performance of the procedure will be undertaken jointly by EDP, Finance and Personnel.

Flow Chart 11

DATA TRANSFER FROM HRMS TO PAYROLL/FINANCE:

Employee Addition data

↓

Primary data regarding any new person joining will be entered into database

↓

Hard copy of the joining order is issued

↓

The data on the new inductee will be transferred electronically to Payroll

↓

Central HRMS section will receive a monthly edit list from Payroll on these new records.

↓

Employee Separation Data

↓

HR executives will issue computerized administrative order through separation module

↓

Limited hard copies of such orders will be generated suitable clearances for final payments given by clearing agencies

↓

Data file containing separation data will be given to Payroll on a fixed day every month

↓

Central HRMS section will receive a monthly edit list on these data from Payroll

Data on Employee Status Change

↓

HR executives will issue the administrative orders through the HRMS module which alters the status of employees

↓

In case of promotion and redesignation, respective personnel executives will generate the DPC/Screening Committee report before the prescribed date of promotion.

↓

Similarly, all concerned HRMS tables will be updated by the users in Personnel department

↓

The delayed cases and correction cases will be fed to Payroll electronically along with the report of the next month.

↓

The Wages sections will not feed any data regarding employee status change. However, discrepancy if any noticed can be referred by Wages section to the concerned HR executive who will take suitable further action.

↓

Central HRMS section will receive a monthly edit list from Payroll containing all details which have been updated.

5.17 Infusing HRMS into the work culture

If the change is not supported and reinforced by culture, it will always require endless extra efforts and it would be difficult to sustain after some lapse of time. The approaches are Matching Reorientation of Structure, Role and Responsibilities, Management Systems, Information System, Education and Training, Reward and Recognition. In this case, these were achieved by the following methods:

Table

	Function	How it was achieved in the case
1	Structure, Role and Responsibilities	A new central HRMS section was formed. Various role clarity guidelines were issued from time to time, specially highlighting the responsibility of HR, Finance and EDP functionaries in each activity.
2	Management Systems	Standard HRMS procedures were covered as SOPs in the ISO 9001: 2000 QMS.
3	Information System	System generated reports were made compulsory for all users.
4	Education and Training	All executives and staff right from the General Manager to lowest level were imparted training. Awareness sessions for top management, cross section employees as well as union officials were also organized.
5	Reward and Recognition	Outstanding cases of operation of HRMS were specially recognized.

Change programs like HRMS are a necessary intervention in the contemporary corporate scenario. The origin of HRM as a management discipline goes back to the Industrial Revolution days, when problems of productivity and human exploitation were to be addressed. Having answered most of these problems, the HR managers in recent past, took up an ambitious role of change agents in modernizing and reorienting the organizational culture towards better competitiveness. The HRM group being in charge of modernization of organization culture should therefore adopt the perspectives of the living concept of our time i.e. Information Technology in a professional manner applying change management skills. Whereas, in HRMS implementation, the HR professionals globally are mostly engrossed about technical supports from software providers; what the HR function needs to strategize, is the change management.

Chapter 6

MODERNIZING THE TRADITIONS

6.1 What Previous Chapters Covered

6.2 A Personal Voice

6.3 Guide Pages for Application

6.1 What Previous Chapters Covered

Arriving now at the last chapter of the book, it is time to recapitulate the points already covered. In the beginning of this book at Chapter-1, we appealed to readers for a more serious interest in Information Technology, its amazing predominance on our culture especially as it works on our mental categories more than on physical abilities. The process of modernization is important to HR and the reader is reminded that the new technology has given rise to a new culture and inadequate attention to this development is making us professionally impoverished. Inadequate imagination on modern culture is already creating problems for HR in IT sector. Further, we noticed that closeness to IT will also enable us to know our employes better. We presented overview of the schema in which the entire book spreads out.

In Chapter-2, we initially spoke about the differences between HR and IT as disciplines, and about why human entities will always escape classical scientific study. They will do so because of their basic existential features like tendency to have freedom of action, sense of moving beyond their present status, uniqueness of being and self-relatedness. All these stand in sharp contrast to the properties of IT which is obsessed to measure and process everything it finds in this universe. Later on we deliberated that there also exists strong similarities in both the perspectives and why HR managers must have a stake in the IT field.

In Chapter-3, we reiterated that technology in different historical stages creates a framework of culture which influences the personality and behaviour of the human actors. Currently IT, the new technology, the upgrader of mind power accordingly creates its own collective unconscious. The task of the HR profession is to be alive to the profile of this new personality and new patterns of behaviour at individual and group level.

generic features of emerging personality are laid down in twin contexts of outer society and modern organizational reality.

In Chapter-4, we come across another meeting point between HR and IT. The crux is that IT can enable the HR manager to know the employee better by capturing the information about him in almost an unlimited manner. We also deal here with designing and developing an HRMS database with features like shared databases with networking, to Expert Systems, removal of barriers between a Generalist and a Specialist, Decision Support Systems, Automatic Tracking and finally to Process Efficiency and Convergence. These issues were deliberated by blending first-hand experience of actual development of a HRMS data to in a very large organization.

In Chapter 5, we deal with transition to HRMS in the format of a change management process. This includes creating a sense of urgency about HRMS, forming of core implementation team by drawing them from HR, Finance and IT, internal collaboration in HR with a shared dream about future, enabling actions for smooth implementation, communication plan for different stake holders, Trials, deadlines, confronting the main obstacles to HRMS, the data verification process and finally infusing HRMS into the HR culture.

6.2 A Personal Voice

To write is to raise a claim for time and attention from the readers. It is also to raise a voice which is personal to the writer. Even though more than half of the pages in this book has been devoted to implementing HRMS, the voice here in this book is based on following five propositions:

1. The first proposition is that modernization is a professional approach that all of us HR practitioners need to adopt into our daily life and work place. What exactly is modernization as a professional approach?

It consists of acquiring a capacity to shift from one perspective to another in human situations, ability to hold all the views in the mind together including the perspective which is taking shape at this moment and in the process to build up an adequate view of *totality* of human group, society and of its components. It is this attitude that should differentiate the Human Resource Practitioner from his technocrat counterpart. In practice the modernization process in HR function is realized by means of following elements.

2. The HR person needs to *practice a little bit of history*. He must have a close look at where does the contemporary society and culture in which his organization is situated, stand in human history? We need to arrange our experiences, data and files which we have been collecting out of our day to day working say in an industry, and analyze as to how does it differ from earlier varieties of social order? There is now more freedom from restrictions of space and time, and freedom from the classical divide between work and leisure. Can this be used to achieve better work-life balance, reduction of stress etc? Within it, what is the meaning of any particular feature for its continuance and for its change? We also need to assess what is the structure of this particular society and community in which our managers and employees live and work? What are its essential components, and how are they related to one another? Control over the 'present' in time and liberation from timings decided by machinery is an important structure of the new technology. Similarly, the progressive culture is enabling transition from particularistic social relationships in social *action* into universalistic ones. Currently, the *secondary groups* are becoming more powerful than the *primary groups*, and

this is facilitated by the technological ability to interact with larger groups even if they are physically far away. The secondary groups in society like discussion forums and associations, are of more intellectual character than the primary groups which basically thrive on emotional bondage. All through in history, man has not been able to tap the full potential of secondary groups of society mainly because of hindrances on information and contacts. The power of secondary groups in social development can be better utilized in the new information culture and with the enabling powers of information technology.

We need to work on, what are the essential features of this period? How does it differ from earlier periods? What are its characteristic ways of making history? A comparative picture for current can be as under:

Earlier times	Now
Reality is primarily based on 19th Century Physics (equilibrium, stability, deterministic, dynamic)	Based on Biology (structure, pattern, self-organization, life cycle). Structure constantly coalescing, decaying, changing
People are identical	People are separate, focus on individual life
If only there is no externality and all had equal abilities, we'd reach our goal.	Externalities and differences become driving force. System constantly unfolding
Elements are individuals and skills	Elements are changing patterns and possibilities
Sees human process as structurally simple	Human processes are inherently complex

3. Keeping a tab on changing profiles of human nature in society and industry is an important task for all of us in HR function. One has to be sensitive to the human types, the varieties of men and women now prevail and varieties which are coming to prevail. In what way are they selected and formed, liberated and repressed, made sensitive and blunted? What kinds of 'human nature' are revealed in the conduct and character we observe around us today at our workplace? For example, absence of a sense of distance in space, frequent mobility and multi-locational behaviour are the new cultural traits in people evidently triggered by the information technology.

The HR practitioner has to be alert about what the meaning of 'human nature' is in each and every sphere of the society that we are examining. Modern life now gets a meaning from its connectivity to several others in this world and the typical Individual and his personality want to be continuously in touch with them.

The advent of information technology in society and business organization has been accompanied by a new type of man with a novel cultural ethos. This new man is rapidly taking shape and the society, economy and culture are fast changing as per his beliefs, values and behaviour patterns. The worldview of the new human type now perhaps looks at the world as a continuous field of ever changing form based on transmission of information. The form of activity that prevails at any one given time reflects a pattern of difference sustained by a particular kind of information exchange. Human beings are engaged in a continual process of interaction and exchange with their context, of receiving, interpreting and acting on the information received and in so doing creating a pattern of information that effects changes in the field as a whole. The question we should ask ourselves is that where as the individuals are turning information processors same has changed the world view of HR functionaries.

4. The HR practitioner needs to place *dissimilar things of this culture together and observe the link.* Put the *structure, sub-structures, functions, subfunctions together, like in a matrix and observe the links.* Look for a new classification, cross classification, skill to make up types, then to search for conditions and consequences of each type. Similarly tabulate the *small and big milieu, the individual, diad, team and higher structures.*

   Job designs become dynamic, open ended, cross functional and project based. Work becomes strategically organized. Cross-functional responsibilities are increasing.

   For example, the main channels of activity are decided by agreed purposes, individuals and projects in the team rather than the hierarchy of the *Organization structure.*

   With the new man and new technology there would be a need to revise all our HR strategies in industrial organizations (same applies to social planner in the context of community work). HR professionals are to work and devise new competency, motivation and culture building methods. The HR Manager has to grasp history, biography and the relations between the two within society. That should be his task and promise.

6.3 Guide Pages for Application

Please refer to appendices.

Appendix 1

JOINING AND INDUCTION OF NEW ENTRANTS

Joining and induction is the first stage of a new employee's career after his recruitment. This event is to store the person's master data into the system and generate a unique employee number which would be used as in HRMS the primary key. In its transactions, this event also sends out the person is details to all the other relevant agencies.

Shared database:	
Data will be in network to which users (Users and Roles) What type of fields/tables of data should be entered/ maintained.	1. Recruitment section 2. Payroll 3. Training Dept 4. HR Dept All not null fields in master employee table would get populated. If Recruitment module is also available, vital data drawn from application form are imported.
In which area extraordinary number of data can be maintained.	If we have a facility for the employees to feed data about himself, we can encourage him to feed in many information beyond our standard requirements.

What should be connectivity, data model, data design (Relationships, Integrity)	Can also provide for becoming a regular employee from a status of trainee or a temporary/casual employee.
Decision support/Expert system	
How decision can be taken at a minimal level	Employee number can be auto generated by a staff in HR department without depending upon Finance department.
How a generalist can do the job of a specialist	Various codes can be entered by the recruitment section which decides his future salary and training.
What decision models can be used	The right to add an employee to the roll of the organization would rest only with the role incharge recruitment. After generation of the employee number, the event of joining can be notified to all other agencies like Payroll, Time Office either through soft or hard mode.
Automatic tracking	
System tells you about important landmarks and deviations	Ensures that no data is lacking before a new employee joins.
Automatic updating of plans	The event of new joining is reflected in all sections automatically.

Process efficiency/Convergence.	
Increase of speed	The new employee need not fill data forms in multiple sections.
Better accuracy in HR measurements/process	Employee's vital data captured once are utilized by multiple sections in HR department. Vital data is used by all concerned in identical form
Cost reduction	Employee data stored at one place and shared by many would be cost efficient.
Paperlessness	No need to share paper report on employee data to many.
Convergence/shared services	After not null fields are entered by Recruitment section, the employee number can be generated through the system.

Appendix 2

SANCTION OF LTC

In most organizations, there is a provision of granting LTC facility to employees. In large organizations this is usually a cumbersome service. HRMS can play an effective role in improving employee satisfaction in this area.

Shared database:	
Data will be in network to which users	HR executives Finance executives
Which major fields/tables of data should be maintained.	LTC control number, Employee number, time block, LTC_type, groups, place of visit, distance, travel mode, bill date, cancel status
In which area extraordinary number of data can be maintained.	
What should be connectivity, data model and data design.	Provides an automatic link between level eligibility and actual sanction of Getyee and mount. Also regularization of advance is easily monitorable.

Decision support/Expert system	
How decision can be taken at a minimal level.	In LTC module, most of the decisions can be taken by the office staff and involvement of executives will not be normally required.
How a generalist can do the job of a specialist.	A generalist staff in HR department can take mostly all decisions which in tradional set up are required to be taken by executives of HR & Finance department.
What decision models can be used.	Designation, grade, employee status, eligibility appears automatic which facilitates LTC decision. Dependents' details are imported from dependent table.
Automatic tracking	
Can provide alerts when an action causes deviations from plan parameters.	Cases of deviations about eligibility conditions surface automatically.
Things tell you about important landmarks and deviations.	Controls can be created about setting limits about number of employees in different areas to be granted LTC in a particular time frame.
Automatic updating of plans.	Eligibility for next LTC is updated. Reminders to defaulting employees is generated.

Process efficiency/Convergence.	
Increase of speed.	Improves by eliminating manual verification , data entry and duplicate data entry.
Better accuracy in HR measurements	
Cost reduction, Paperlessness	Practically can be managed by only one copy of paper, document i.e. employees application from LTC.
Convergence	Postponement, cancellation of LTC can be handled by the same system.

Appendix 3

EMPLOYEE SEPARATIONS

Every organization has a notified age for retirement. On attaining this age the employee is separated from the roll of the organization. There are also cases like Resignation, Death and Voluntary Retirement which causes separation from the organization. The separation module in HRMS enables the formation of a new separated status to the employees and facilitates payment of final dues to him.

Shared database:	
Data will be in network to which users	Unit HR executives Final settlement cell
What fields/tables of data should be maintained.	Separation type Separation date
In which area extraordinary number of data can be maintained.	Though on separation, an employee departs from organizations roll, his data is kept stored for various future uses. As such only his status is changed to separated and a complete database of separated employees is maintained.

What should be connectivity, data model, data design.	Separation type and Separation dates are maintained as per case. This separation status enables HRMS to deactivate the process application for working employees.
Decision support/Expert system	
How decision can be taken at a minimal level.	Clerical efforts are minimized by way of computerized generation of report. Dependence on paper records however contain as per legal requirement
How a generalist can do the job of a specialist.	Inclusion of various internal checks would ensure that system verifies eligibilities for resignation and VR.
What decision models can be used.	Actual financial payment is released only when the status is separation, and all designated agencies indicate their clearance.
Automatic tracking	
Can provide alerts when an action causes deviations from plan parameters.	Payment release function can get alert when clearances from all agencies are not available.
Things tell you about important landmarks and deviations.	Follow up with agencies who have not sent their clearances can be enabled.

Automatic updating of plans.	In case of retirement, status of the employee will automatically change to retirement once the system date indicates the required years without waiting for any manual interventions.
Process efficiency/Convergence.	
Increase of speed.	System communicates the changed status to all concerned agencies faster and more reliable than the manual mode.
Better accuracy in HR measurements.	
Cost reduction, Paperlessness	Since separation is a fundamental event, it normally involves communication and feedback to a very large number of agencies.
Convergence	

Appendix 4

MULTIPURPOSE EMPLOYEE INFORMATION FORM

A multipurpose employee information form is a normal function in any HRMS. The form will flow the employee's vital information for the use of executives and staff of HR deptt, as well as self check by employee themselves.

Shared database:	
Data will be in network to which users (Users and Roles).	1. All members of HR dept 2. Employees for self viewing 3. Shared services centers
What fields/tables of data should be maintained.	Employees name, sex, category, department, zone, section, designation, working status, qualification, governing rules, basic pay, other pays, date of birth, date of joining, grade, blood group, local address, permanent address, list of family members, status (working/separated), status change date (if separated), and more. (pls see page-for a longer list of fields)

In which area extraordinary number of data can be maintained.	If there is a self service facility, everytime an employee queries about something, we can have a system of asking some additional information about himself. This way information on each employee will grow with each passing day.
What should be connectivity, data model, unique table, data design (Relationships, Integrity).	It's a snap shot view of employee's vital information. No transaction takes place here for change of data.
Decision support/Expert system	
How decision can be taken at a minimal level.	Employee can view all the personal information and there would not be any need to go over to the Personnel Office to enquire about it.
How a generalist can do the job of a specialist.	Eligibility flags for various fringe benefits and payments can also be displayed.
What decision models can be used.	This can enable the employee to make an appraisal about various fringe benefits and misc payments (advances etc) for which he is eligible. This in turn can take him to a self service stage.

Automatic tracking	
Can provide alerts when an action causes deviations from plan parameters.	For the personnel executives, various alerts can be provided in this module. For example, alert about an employee who is retiring in the next six months.
Things tell you about important landmarks and deviations.	When self-viewing is allowed, the employee will also get alerted about various things.
Automatic updating of plans.	For example, if you plan to have a special interaction program for employees retiring in the next six months, the same can be reported in regular periods.
Process efficiency/Convergence.	
Increase of speed.	Employee is informed instantly and no need to move to various tables in the office building or waiting for a particular clerk.
Better accuracy in HR measurements.	Calculations precise and no scope for human error.
Cost reduction	Less staff and stationery.
Paperlessness	No need to dispatch papers from one office to another.
Convergence/shared services	You can take a decision on employee services from any of the user terminals instead of a particular office.

Appendix 5

EMPLOYEE DISCIPLINE

With all the best efforts on performance management and counselling, indiscipline does take place in industrial organizations. There are two reasons to maintain this data in HRMS. One is maintaining the history of events so that we can decide for harsher penalty if the indiscipline is repeated. Second one is to regulate his remunerations as penalty.

Shared database:	
Data will be in network to which users.	• HR executives • Payroll
What fields/tables of data should be maintained.	Misconduct type, action-type, Days of absence, enquiry officer name, enquiry date, penalty type, penalty grade, penalty pay, date from, date to.
In which area extraordinary number of data can be maintained.	All details of disciplinary action with its linkage with pay and career growth can be maintained all through the career as a single pool of information.

What should be connectivity, data model, data design.	The module can be run again and again as a new step arises in the disciplinary process. Thus discipline module provides inputs to pay and promotion tables.
Decision support/Expert system	
How decision can be taken at a minimal level.	
How a generalist can do the job of a specialist.	Many of the legal implications of steps of disciplinary action like departmental enquiry and imposition of penalty can be taken care by the system.
What decision models can be used.	Data is transferred to Payroll and promotion tables at the appropriate stage.
Automatic tracking	
Can provide alerts when an action causes deviations from plan parameters.	Alerts can be sent to all other modules as to the disciplinary status of the employees so that if required differential decisions can be taken.
Things tell you about imp landmarks and deviations.	Reminders are created if any stage of the process takes more time than the norm as per Standard Operating Procedures.

Automatic updating of plans	Pre-penalty status is restored automatically as the system date equals the terminal date of the penalty.
Process efficiency/Convergence.	
Increase of speed	Communication to multiple users and Payroll is faster.
Better accuracy in HR measurements	
Cost reduction	
Paperlessness	Data transfer to end use in Payroll takes place through system. No separate process is required to be undertaken for restoring the pre-penalty status after the time is over.
Convergence	

Appendix 6

MULTISKILL TRAINING

Multiskilling is a major OD (Organization Development) intervention in any organization. Its principles are threefold. Each employee must learn a new skill. After acquiring the skill, the evaluated employee should be placed in a borderless set up. Once the above two conditions are met, the employee should be rewarded appropriately.

Shared database:	
Data will be in network to which users.	All HR executives
What fields/tables of data should be maintained.	Skill codification data Individual skill profile
In which area extra-ordinary number of data can be maintained.	Data on varieties of skill like skills the employee had prior to his recruitment, skills acquired through the in-company training institute, skills learnt through experience and skills required to be acquired in future, can be stored.

What should be connectivity, data model, data design.	There would be two tables namely skill code master and skill profile. Skill code can contain digits for both the functional skill like operator, welder, fitter as well as the code of the department where the skill is used. The skill profile can capture all the data regarding skills of the employee as he acquires them as well management plan for future skill identified for him.
Decision support/Expert system	
How decision can be taken at a minimal level.	
How a generalist can do the job of a specialist.	For transfers and redeployment the skill of employee can be matched with job profile of the new location.
What decision models can be used.	For manpower planning lot of matching skill can be generated.
Automatic tracking	
Can provide alerts when an action causes deviations from plan parameters.	Various alerts can be developed for effective monitoring of the process of acquisition of new skills as well rewarding employees as they do the same.

Things tell you about imp landmarks and deviations.	
Automatic updating of plans.	Annual plan for skill development can be updated.
Process efficiency/Convergence.	
Increase of speed.	
Better accuracy in HR measurements.	Skill inventory is available in a standardized manner.
Cost reduction,	
Paperlessness	
Convergence	

Appendix 7

TRANSFER OF EMPLOYEES

Transfer is a regular event in a multilocation, multi-department and large organizations. The movement of the employees to different departments, sections are needed to be recorded. This is required so that he starts to earn the remunerations of his new positions and at the same time his career history is archived.

Types of transfer are normally of following three types:

1. Transfers outside the location.
2. Transfers to another department in the same location.
3. Transfers to another job in the same location.

Shared database:	
Data will be in network to which users	Finance HR executives
What fields/tables of data should be maintained.	A new transfer table is required with following major fields: Emp no, old dept, old section, old designation, date_of_transfer, date of release from old dept, joining date, new dept, new section, new designation, new Payroll bill no.

In which area extraordinary number of data can be maintained.	Integrated, updated view of job rotations during a career.
What should be connectivity, data model, data design.	The form's relevant fields would be filled by releasing department and the rest by the new department.
Decision support/Expert system	
How decision can be taken at a minimal level.	A staff in HR department can take many decisions in the new department which in traditional set up are required to be taken by an HR executive.
How a generalist can do the job of a specialist.	
What decision models can be used.	Rights to handle the data of the employee in old department are automatically transferred to the new department.
Automatic tracking	
Can provide alerts when an action causes deviations from plan parameters.	Receiving departments gets an alert instantaneously as the person is released from the old department.
Things tell you about imp landmarks and deviations.	Releasing department also gets an alert if the process is not completed in the new department within the time limit.

Automatic updating of plans.	Transferee's current profile is updated automatically and the old status is sent to the history table.
Process efficiency/Convergence.	
Increase of speed.	Information of release is available through system to all concerned instantaneously.
Better accuracy in HR measurements.	Keeps day to day update about number of employees in any department.
Cost reduction,	
Paperlessness	
Convergence	

Appendix 8

PROMOTIONS

Shared database:	
Data will be in network to which users.	HR executive in the zone of promotion.
What fields/tables of data should be maintained.	Promotion history table to be maintained.
In which area extraordinary number of data can be maintained.	
What should be connectivity, data model, data design.	Because of well known complexity of promotion decisions, this module is linked to several tables including appraisal, seniority, sanction posts, vacancy etc.
Decision support/Expert system Computer application that enhances a person's or group's ability to make decisions	
How decision can be taken at a minimal level.	Fixation of post-promotion revised pay is done through system.
How a generalist can do the job of a specialist.	
What decision models can be used.	

Automatic tracking	
Can provide alerts when an action causes deviations from plan parameters.	Alerts on list of employees eligible for promotion on any particular period. Alerts when promotion parameters are not met, for example, when appraisal rating is below the minimum required.
Things tell you about important landmarks and deviations.	
Automatic updating of plans.	
Process efficiency/Convergence.	
Increase of speed.	
Better accuracy in HR measurements.	
Cost reduction	
Paperlessness	Hard copy reports would not be required from agencies like vigilance, appraisal or manpower.
Convergence/shared services	

Appendix 9

PAYROLL AND SALARY ADMINISTRATION

The dictionary of computer contains a term called 'convergence', which means coming together of dissimilar things. Its some thing like in orchestra where different notes come together to produce a single music. The HR-Payroll technology is something like a convergence. Here physically though Personnel and Finance exist as two separate departments, in implementation they act seamlessly like they are one agency.

When an employee is promoted, promotion decision is taken in HR department, his increase in salary is also decided in HR department. HR usually prepares a report for departmental promotion committee on which decisions on promotion are taken. Thereafter, HR issues an administrative order which is sent to Finance carrying the promotion decision and fixation of the revised salary of the employee. The Finance used to recheck the calculations, feed the data into their PayRoll system, and just before salary day used to send the advice to the employee's bank accordingly.

Payroll and salary administration is a method core to functioning of HR department dealing with disbursement of monthly salary to employees. The process consists of calculation of different components of pay, allowances as well as varieties of deductions. Administering salary is a very sensitive (it directly affects employee satisfaction) as well as complex function (as it deals with close working with finance functions).

Shared database:	
Data will be in network to which users.	• Unit HR offices • Central HRMS • Payroll • Time Office
What fields/tables of data should be maintained.	Attendance, various types of leave, absence, shifts, weekly off.
In which area extraordinary number of data can be maintained.	Sources of attendance and leave data along with dates
What should be connectivity, data model, data design.	Linking attendance data with employee's salary eligibility and function to electronic transfer to individual bank account.
Decision support/Expert system	
How decision can be taken at a minimal level.	Final salary account can be decided by a staff.
How a generalist can do the job of a specialist.	If principle of salary and promotion, increment amount, dates, deductions applicable are embedded in the program, general list staff can enable the right calculation.
What decision models can be used	Financial transaction is limited by the list which is in employee master. (After deduction are made, the amount is automatically transferred to respective heads).

Automatic tracking	
Can provide alerts when an action causes deviations from plan parameters.	Alerts if net pay is exceeding a maximum or minimum predetermined level.
Things tell you about important landmarks and deviations	
Automatic updating of plans	
Process efficiency/Convergence.	
Increase of speed	Digital transfer from Timekeeping to HR to Payroll saves time of data entry at multiple points.
Better accuracy in HR measurements/process	Reduction in manual data entry helps in better data accuracy.
Cost reduction	Reduction in data entry entitles reduced staff
Paperlessness	Paper transfer from Time keeping to HR to Finance is reduced substantially.
Convergence	Enables several forms of data analysis about employees.

Appendix 10

COMPETENCY MAPPING AND SKILL INVENTORY

Competency has been defined as any underlying characteristic of an individual resulting in superior performance on the job reflected in a pattern of actions (skills), thoughts (knowledge) and feelings (attitudes) in the individual. Competency mapping is a process of identifying key competencies for a particular job and incorporating those competencies throughout the various processes (i.e. job evaluation, training, recruitment) of the organization.

The use of competencies can include: assessment during recruitment, through specific work-based exercises and relevant, validated, psychometric tests; assessment during further development; as a profile during assessment to guide future development needs; succession planning and promotion; organizational development analysis. A major use of competency data is to identify training needs and deploy training events to improve the gap in the profile.

<table>
<tr><th colspan="2">Shared database:</th></tr>
<tr><td>Data will be in network to which users (Users and Roles)</td><td>Recruitment section
Job rotation Section
Training Engineers
Manpower Planning Section</td></tr>
</table>

What fields/tables of data should be maintained.	Roles, competency models, skill codes, knowledge codes, attitude codes, assessment scores.
In which area extraordinary number of data can be maintained.	The competency model can be continuously enriched by adding detailed multiple components to the skill, knowledge and attitude.
What should be the linkages.	In a large, complex and multi-department organization it is necessary that the competency data is stored in the computer system for enabling varied uses that competency is utilized for. As such different modules like transfer, salary administration, training need generation, promotion, career plan can be effectively linked.
Decision support/Expert system	
How decision can be taken at a minimal level.	Various types of training needs can be generated by any training coordinator.
How a generalist can do the job of a specialist.	List of possible successor with desirable competency to a separating executive can be drawn out by HR officers.

What decision models can be used.	System can provide filters of age, qualification and competency to arrive at a pool of eligible population to succeed to any given role.
Automatic tracking	
Can provide alerts when an action causes deviations from plan parameters.	You can get an alert when an incumbent with wide deviations against competency model is in place for some period of time.
Things tell you about important landmarks and deviations.	When we have requirement for a Job Rotation, the competency data can very easily point out persons for rotation in matching positions. Similarly, when there is manpower requirement for a new project, this information can be efficiently utilized.
Automatic updating of plans.	Succession plans are updated on real time basis.
Process efficiency/Convergence.	
Increase of speed.	Annual Training Plan can be generated immediately from the competency database.
Better accuracy in HR measurements.	Measurement of competency levels in various components can be very accurate.
Cost reduction.	Less manpower. Less paper records.

Paper efficient set-ups	No need to keep piles of paper versions of competency data.
Convergence	Processes of performance management, salary administration, succession management and training are combined in this process.

Appendix 11

ISO 9001 : 2008 WITH HR AND QMS

Customer focus and Continual Improvement are the two fundamental precepts of ISO 9001. In practice the standard requires formulation of various manuals and SOPs (Standard Operating Procedures). Calculation of customer satisfaction index as well. In the QMS of HR, employees, employee information and line authorities are normally taken as customers.

Shared database:	
Data will be in network to which users	All addresses in the document control procedure.
What fields/tables of data should be maintained.	All indices mentioned in the quality objectives.
In which area extraordinary number of data can be maintained.	All transaction dates which are relevant to indicate compliance/non-compliance of SOPs.
What should be the linkages	SOP wise linkage with various transactions.
Decision support/Expert system	
How decision can be taken at a minimal level	Measurement and analysis of events can be done by staff themselves.
How a generalist can do the job of a specialist	One can know compliance with SOPs without consulting any functional expert.

What decision models can be used.	One can plan for improvements in all procedures by efficient realtime data analysis
Automatic tracking	
Can provide alerts when an action causes deviations from plan parameters.	Forms can send out alerts when SOPs are violated.
Things tell you about important landmarks and deviations.	Transactions causing deviations which are mandatorily not allowed can be prevented.
Automatic updating of plans.	Applicable to quality plans. Also online maintenance of procedures makes it easy to revise the plans.
Process efficiency/Convergence	
Increase of speed	Evidences of transactions can be generated automatically. These records can be displayed with ease at the time of audits.
Better accuracy in HR measurements	Online generation of data makes them more accurate.
Cost reduction	Less manpower needed for Internal audit.
Paperlessness	With suitable changes in document procedure SOPs and data can be permitted to be kept in digital mode.
Convergence	Better alignment with satisfaction of internal customers of HR.

A SURVEY

Objectives:

1. To identify different types of information pertaining to HR which should be stored and processed in Computer System
2. To identify functions of HR department which should be covered by computer application so as to reap the benefits of speed, accuracy, storage capacity and automation

Instructions:

- ✓ There are 3 subjective questions and they have to be answered as precisely and accurately as possible.
- ✓ There are some objective questions also. Each of these have 4 alternative answers: 'already', 'must be', 'can be', and 'need not be'; whichever one you feel is the answer should be *tick marked* in the provided box against it.
- ✓ There is no correct answer as such.

Kindly specify your

Designation : ______________________________

Department : ______________________________

Section : ______________________________

Grade : ______________________________

Yrs. of Service : ______________________________

1. Give your answers for the following:

Sl. No.	Functional Areas of HR	Already Computerized	Must Be Computerized	Can Be Computerized	Need Not Be Computerized
1.	Manpower Planning				
2.	Organizational Structure				
3.	Interpersonal Relationships				
4.	Motion, Time & Work Study				
5.	Recruitment & Selection Process				
6.	Placement, Induction & Orientation				
7.	Promotion & Transfer Process				
8.	Separation Process				
9.	Competency Assessment & Training				

Sl. No.	Functional Areas of HR	Already Computerized	Must Be Computerized	Can Be Computerized	Need Not Be Computerized
10.	Evaluation of Job & Performance Appraisals				
11.	Wage & Salary Programmes				
12.	Incentive & Compensation Plans/ Fringe Benefits				
13.	Motivating People				
14.	Development of Safety & Health Techniques and Services				
15.	Employee Counselling				
16.	Recreation Facility				
17.	Providing Education & Employee Services				
18.	Grievance Handling				

19.	Maintaining Discipline in the Organization				
20.	Developing Reward & Punishment System				
21.	Complying with Labour Laws				
22.	Maintaining Payrolls				
23.	Maintaining Industrial Relations:-	---------	---------	---------	--------
	a. Collective Bargaining				
	b. Joint Consultation				
	c. Participative Decision Making				
24.	Making Personnel Audits & Research				
25.	Suggestions & Saving Plans Provision				

Sl. No.	Functional Areas of HR	Already Computerized	Must Be Computerized	Can Be Computerized	Need Not Be Computerized
26.	HR Administration of Leave etc.				
27.	Organizational Climate Survey				
28.	OD Interventions				

2. Give your answers as per the actual working of Personnel Department:

Sl. No.	Employee's Information	Already Included	Must Be Included	Can Be Included	Need Not Be Included
1.	Personal Information				
2.	Address				
3.	Grade History				
4.	Educational Qualification of Children				
5.	Accident Details				

6.	Nominee Details				
7.	Reward & Punishment Details				
8.	Spouse Details				
9.	Cost of Living				
10.	Standard of Living				
11.	Learning Capacity				
12.	Birthdays of Family Members				
13.	Dependent's Details				
14.	Career Profile				
15.	Stress Level				
16.	Motivational Level				

Sl. No.	Employee's Information	Already Included	Must Be Included	Can Be Included	Need Not Be Included
17.	Intelligence Quotient				
18.	Emotional Quotient				
19.	Spiritual quotient				
20.	Family Planning				
21.	Court Cases Details				
22.	Blood Donations				
23.	Employee's Attitude towards Life and Work				

24.	Attitude of Parents towards the Employee				
25.	Felicitations Received Other than Work Area				
26.	Detention Details				
27.	Employment Details before SAIL				
28.	Brief Family History				
29.	Employee's Likes & Dislikes				
30.	Personality Traits				
31.	Role Model				

Sl. No.	Employee's Information	Already Included	Must Be Included	Can Be Included	Need Not Be Included
32.	Leave Details				
33.	Membership of Associations				
34.	Hobbies/Extra Curricular Activities				
35.	Health History				
36.	Habits				
37.	Ambition/Aim in Life				
38.	Educational Qualification				
39.	Technical Qualification				
40.	Skills				
41.	Loan Details				

42.	Salary Details				
43.	Brief History About Peer Group				
44.	Brief Biographical Details				
45.	Contacts in Emergency				
46.	Transfers & Promotions				
47.	HRA Details				
48.	Separations				
49.	Disciplinary Actions				
50.	Redeployment				
51.	Job Preferences				

Please give your valuable suggestions for the following questions:

3. What kind of HR related information is being stored in the computer system used by you?

   a. ______________________________

   b. ______________________________

   c. ______________________________

   d. ______________________________

   e. ______________________________

4. What characteristics of employee according to you should be available to the management for a wholesome HR related functioning?

   a. ______________________________

   b. ______________________________

   c. ______________________________

   d. ______________________________

   e. ______________________________

5. What do you feel can be further done to improve the speed, accuracy and automation in the working of Personnel Department?

   a. ______________________________

   b. ______________________________

   c. ______________________________

   d. ______________________________

   e. ______________________________

BIBLIOGRAPHY

Becker, B. E., Huselid, M. A., & Ulrich, D. The HR scorecard: Linking People, Strategy, and Performance. Boston: Harvard Business School Press, 2001

Brown John Seely and Duguid Paul, The Social Life of Information, Harvard Business School Press, 1999

Cascio, W. F., Costing Human Resources: The financial impact of behavior in organizations (4th ed.). Cincinnati, OH: South-Western College, 2000.

Collison Jessica, HR Technology Survey Report. Society for Human Resource Management, SHRM Research Department, Alexandria, 2005

Davis, W. S., Systems Analysis and Design: A structured approach. MA: Addison,1983.

Durant, Will. The Story of Philosophy. New York :Washington Square Press, 1962.

Fitz-Enz, J., How to Measure Human Resource Management (3rd ed.). New York:McGraw-Hill, 2002.

Gates Bill. The Road Ahead. London. Penguin Books, 1996

Gates Bill. Business @ Speed of Thought. London. Warner Books, 2000

Huselid, M. A., Becker, B. E., & Beatty, R. W., The Workforce Scorecard: Managing Human Capital to Execute Strategy. Boston: Harvard Business School Press, 2005.

Fromm, Erich. Beyond the Chain of Illusions - My Encounter with Marx and Freud. London : Abacus, 1983

Kavanagh, Michael J., Outlines & Highlights for Human Resource Information Systems, Lightning Source Inc, 2010

Martin, Graeme et al. Technology, Outsourcing & Transforming HR. Butterworth-Heinemann, 2008

Sartre, Jean Paul., Existentialism is a Humanism: Existentialism from Dostovesky to Sartre. Ed. Kaufmann Walter. New York: Median, 1956

Schramm Jennifer, HR Technology Competencies: New Roles for HR Professionals. Society for Human Resource Management, SHRM Research Department, Alexandria, 2006

Shrinivasan, MN., Caste in Modern India and other essays. Asia Publishing House, (1962)

Waldrop Mitchell M., Complexity. The Emerging Science at the Edge of Order and Chaos, New York, Simon Schuster paperbacks, 1992